Faking It In France

Karen Bates

Wl   bo   fe, some names
ha   ch   entity of those
in\

SU
COUN

Published in 2012 by FeedARead.com Publishing – Arts Council funded

Faking It In France Copyright © Karen Bates 2012.

First Edition

A CIP catalogue record for this title is available from the British Library.

Cover Illustration Copyright © 2012 by Karen Bates

Cover Design Copyright © 2012 by Karen Bates

Book Design and Production by Karen Bates and Sarah Reeves

Editing by Karen Bates and Sarah Reeves

Author Photograph by Ashley Reeves

Poetry by Karen Bates

Find out more about the author and upcoming books online: www.karenbates.moonfruit.com or on Twitter: @KarenBates64

Dedication and Acknowledgement

Dedicated to Sarah, Ashley, and never forgotten Matthew.

My thanks go to Sarah for all her patience, support and hard work. Joanne Rees for editing and copious cups of tea provided by Alan.

To Adele Dacre for bringing to life my idea for the book cover with her wonderful artistic flair. A big thank you to Brian Douglas and Chloe for support, formatting and editing work.

To Ashley for his photos and love. My Mum and Dad for their continuous help and guidance. Friends and family, Especially Sally, for their crazy stories and belief in me. Lastly without who none of this would have been possible my wonderful husband Terry who very rarely told me to shut up going on about my book and will be very pleased to see it finally in print. Hoping then I might talk about something else, but then, there is always the sequel...

Contents

Prologue

You have to love yourself more
love yourself the most.
No one else will do it
no one else will come close.
Look deep inside your soul
take time to know your brain
and when you think you have it sussed
it's time to try again...

They lie to you. All those tantalising dwellings on their attractive web sites are a seduction technique. They must be, as after we told the dishevelled, chain-smoking estate agent, Monsieur Albert, our budget he doubled over with hysterical laughter. Picking himself up off the floor, he erupted into an involuntary fit of gasping and nearly let go of his cigarette. Regaining composure, he re-lit the soggy paper and tobacco he was gripping for dear life between his tainted lips, saying, "Oh you Ingleesh, you are so 'ilarious!"

My husband Terry and I, together with the children from my previous marriage, had come to Normandy to view houses. We were enthusiastic to see the enchanting properties that you get advertised for sale. Cottages with flowers round the door, birds singing their hearts out in the trees, cows in the field and all yours for just ten thousand euros.

Careering along the Normandy countryside, flying past flower-filled hedgerows in Monsieur Albert's ancient, creaking Citroen (which smelt like the inside of his tobacco pouch) we felt that we had viewed every old house that hadn't been inhabited since Marie-Antoinette met her fate at the guillotine. Ramshackle, isolated cowsheds would make, according to Monsieur Albert, "wonderful 'oliday 'omes," as he knew that "the Ingleesh just adore zee rural 'ouses."

Bidding him "bon soir", we finally returned, weary and disillusioned, back to the cottage where we were staying and I reached for the corkscrew.

It had not been as easy as we thought it would be. I was afraid that if our savings weren't converted into bricks and mortar soon, Terry would squander them on alcohol, motorbikes and even more Star Trek paraphernalia. Where was our dream French manoir that all the TV programmes had promised us?

"Let's up our budget," I impetuously announced, opening a second bottle of wine, "and why not make it a permanent move! After all, Sid lives here!"

"Your brother still doesn't have an inside toilet after three years,' Terry reminded me, 'and he asked you to bring twenty tins of baked beans."

A little domestic upheaval wouldn't put me off, and I didn't eat that many beans.

So the next day saw us turning up in Monsieur Albert's nicotine-stained office to impart the news to him. Obviously, he was delighted – we could almost see the euro signs going round in his eyes as he reached for his cigarettes and car keys. He enthusiastically told us that we had "la bonne chance, as a luverly 'ouse ad just come up for sale that very morning." Hmmm...

As soon as we approached the property down the picturesque, winding French lane and followed the rainbow to its end (it really was at the end of the rainbow) I knew that this would be our new home. I don't know why, I am not usually that fanciful. I mean, I would always reserve judgement and have a good look inside at least. With this house I didn't need to – I just knew, and I think my husband agreed. Even the children, who were keenly exploring, looked relieved that we might find happiness again in a new home.

With granite lintels above the shuttered windows and a sprawling wisteria clinging to the stone walls, it looked perfect. Inside, it was full of character with a huge inglenook fireplace dominating the lounge, beams the size of ancient oak trees and a kitchen bigger than our entire home in England.

It wasn't however, any of these things that made me feel so inexplicably drawn to it – I really couldn't explain why I felt this way. It was our first wedding anniversary that day so I put it down to my feelings of joy and contentment (and, it being my third marriage, I was secretly relieved we had made it this far). Once we had got rid of the dead rabbit carcass and installed a cooker, I knew we could transform the neglected house into our dream home.

At the end of the tour I turned to Monsieur Albert, who was again re-lighting the crumpled cigarette he appeared to have been smoking since the day before, and stated that this was "the" house and we would like to buy it. I think he must have thought his boat had come in, as within five minutes of arriving we (well me, really) had agreed to purchase the property. I didn't even think about the consequences.

As we stood on the gravel driveway of what was to be our new home, 'Hôtel Marion', the sun tipped its head through the mist and the evocative smell of wood-smoke hung in the air. The true splendour of the house was revealed just long enough for us to know that this was a truly captivating moment, and one that would change our lives forever.

Back in England, we had been shoe-horned into a tiny terraced house which was bursting at the seams. We had a parking attendant living on one side, and three boisterous children on the other. We had been sandwiched in suburbia. The final straw had been when we returned from a weekend away, only to discover our DIY mad neighbour had erected yet another monstrous shed.

"It'll be so he can segregate that randy rooster of his!" Terry exclaimed.

Hôtel Marion, on the other hand, sat proudly in its own land and there was parking for any number of vehicles. The only neighbours were the inquisitive cows who were poking their snot-slathered faces through the hedge, keen to make our acquaintance. It was idyllic, peaceful and serene. It was impossible not to fall in love and I would be free to park anywhere I wanted. I would no longer have to face the glaring stares from my neighbour for transgressing his kerbstones and, hopefully, the only cock waking me in the morning would be my husband's.

Time for a Change

Ten years later, Terry and I were still married, living at Hôtel Marion, and by some miracle, my 17-year-old son Ashley had settled in very well at school and relished living here. Terry had a thriving business as a carpenter and had even built his own home cinema.

It was me. I was the problem. I was bored and homesick. The novelty had worn off. My French dream had not materialised.

I tried to find work, but it was impossible. There weren't enough jobs for the French, so why would they employ me?

I was Terry's secretary and often worked alongside him, usually cleaning up the mess he had made. He was an artisan who charged "artisan prices". The clients weren't too happy when the wife turned up – it just didn't look professional. So I was stuck at home dealing with the paperwork. With Ashley at school all week and Sarah at university in London, even the role of a mother was restricted. I was in that not so enviable position of being a lady of leisure.

Alone and adrift, I was living in a farmhouse in the middle of a field. I felt like Hugh Grant in that film when he says "all men are an island" but my island wasn't Ibiza, it was more like Alcatraz.

Normandy was light years behind England and you couldn't even get a decent Indian take-away. Seriously, I had to do something if I was to keep myself from going insane and to enjoy what we had. There was a large chunk absent in my life, a void. I had sentenced myself to solitary confinement and I was stuck in a charming, secluded farmhouse in the middle of nowhere. I was getting lonelier by the day and the bottle of gin on the sideboard had started to look very inviting. I had to change, fill the void with something, anything - but not the gin, well not at eleven in the morning anyway.

I had been friendly with my elderly French neighbours until we had exhausted every topic of conversation that was possible with my inadequate schoolgirl French. I had also made countless friends with British people that had emigrated here, only to get close and then lose them as they failed to find work and ended up going back to England. This had been so painful the last time – I was fed up with having to say goodbyes.

I had my teenage son and his French girlfriend, but when they were home they only emerged from his room at feeding times. She never turned up with a coat, so I had come to assume that she was not the outdoor type. My lovely, amusing, Star Trek-mad husband spent most of his evenings in his cinema watching Captain Kirk and other assorted science fiction. Then there was my crazy mixed-up dog, which had a tendency to spend all day in the shower because he was afraid of just about everything – the hunter's guns, thunderstorms, loud bangs, the dishwasher, the hoover, even his own shadow. When he did come out of hiding, his panache for stealing was actually something to be admired. His favourite loot was shoes, socks, cushions, bath mats, remote controls and my glasses, but nothing was really off limits if he fancied it.

I was stagnant. I had to do something, anything, to get me out of this rut. I had got myself into this mess after all. Terry, trying to be helpful, and ever-keen to find a solution (aren't all men?), threw in a few ideas.

"You could join a club – Mrs Brown goes to gymnastics – or you could try and get a job. Mrs Foster signed-on the pôle-emploi and they sent her on a course to teach her how to write her c.v."

This didn't fill me with any inspiration, particularly when he reminded me that there was always the ex-pat's society…

"Okay then, if you really want something to do, go and paint the attic bedroom or clear out the garage, or you can always come and work with me – there's plenty of cleaning up to do!"

I bet there is, I thought, and started to sulk.

"Or you could write a diary,' he sniggered, 'you know a sort of Captain's log.' Then he shot off to his cinema to watch Star Trek before I could hassle him any further.

I think he meant it as a joke, or to shut me up. He was desperate to get in to his den that night – my Mum had just sent him some Deep Space Nine DVDs she had found in the Age Concern shop. I do wish she wouldn't encourage him.

11

So, as I sat in the deserted kitchen on my own with a packet of Marlboros and a dripping tap for company, I started thinking. This could be it, it could work. Why not keep a journal? I might at least be able to do that. I could ramble on about life in Normandy – what the dog had stolen and eaten today, what my Mum and Dad were up to and how they were managing with my poor old Gran. I could whine on and generally have a good old moan and at the end of it, use it as proof to my husband why we should sell up and go back to England.

There Must be More to Life

9th November

Walked the dog, checked my e-mails. Nothing. Well, one from the Bournemouth Scientology Mission and another one from Amazon. Had a look on Facebook as usual. Again, nothing. Cleaned the cooker, did the washing, went shopping.

10th November

Walked the dog (even though he didn't want to go) and checked my e-mails (just Brittany Ferries special offers and a reminder from my daughter to bring her some tobacco over at Christmas). Had a look on Facebook, Sarah had got another parking ticket! Cleaned the bathroom, did a bit of gardening, posted the bills.

11th November

Walked the dog (twice), did the hoovering, cleaned out the fridge. Checked my e-mails – special offer on kettles at Mr. Good Deal! Had a look on Facebook and I found a new friend request – YES, YES, YES! I responded. Someone is actually contacting me! She is the owner of my dog's puppy – what a shame she lives so far away in Munich and is German. No matter, a friend is a friend and I'm really in no position to be choosy.

12th November

Walked the dog, made the dinner, had a lie down. Nothing to do, so e-mailed my new Facebook friend some photos of my dog Sam, her dog's Dad.

13th November

Felt like doing nothing, so put my feet up and watched Jeremy Kyle. At this rate, I would surely end up on Prozac.

This was not going well. In fact, looking back at what I had written, I actually felt worse. It sort of reinforced my mundane life. If I didn't get some inspiration soon, I would end up doing gymnastics with a load of 60-something Norman housewives, or joining the ex-pats.

Then, as if by magic, it came to me. I was clearing out a drawer when inside I found an old diary full of poems, recipes and notes that I had written years ago. The pages were full of angst and heartache written when I was going through a particularly painful time. As I started to read them I was amazed - I had done it before and I could do it again.

A New Start

What went wrong?

Why did it snap?

Who pulled the trigger and let off the cap?

Emptying out all of me

For the whole bloody world and his wife to see.

I was so naive so tucked away

And now I am living emotions day to day.

This wasn't how it was supposed to be

Husband and wife to eternity

But he did the dirty, the shit hit the fan

And I'm a real woman not some martyred man

I've found my true self, been shocked what I have seen,

But also I like it, it is the real me

She smiles, looks around her, sees beauty and praise

Sees real people not players playing plays

Is confident courageous not frightened or scared

And will live her true life with people who care

Give love and compassion and feel from the heart

It was worth it to get here this is my new start.

So, no more messing about, no more putting it off, no more self pity – my proper journal would start here and at the end of the month I would sit down and review it. I could then chart my progress and see if it was working.

Captains Log

December 2nd

"Everything is going well with the Christmas preparations," my mother gushed excitedly on the phone. It's like a military operation for her and usually starts around September when she announces that she has bought and wrapped all of her presents. This is guaranteed to send me into a spin of inadequacy and irritation that I am not that organized, ugh!

"I have ordered the turkey from Bob the butcher you know, my second cousin, he's got the shop in the Village, always gets us a lovely bird and your Dad bought Sarah a George Foreman grill at a bargain price," she continued without a breath, "your Dad has joined the Co-op."

Is it like the Freemasons? I wondered.

"So he got 5% off and as it was 10% discount day as well, he got 15% off in total, a real result. Your dad says it's about time Sarah started cooking, she can't live on fags and fresh air all her life!" She laughed.

Mum had been to see Gran, who was on top form, and looking forward to seeing us all at Christmas.

"She really perked up, said she wasn't sure if she would manage to get out of bed, but she was a lot livelier, and no swearing it was a pleasure to visit her. She looked quite her old self and really energized," Mum added. After being in bed for nearly two years I think I would be as well. Gran wanted to know why people kept telling her Grandad was dead,

"Who would say a thing like that? He comes and sees me every morning, and then he's off, and I don't know where he gets to all day," she complained.

Mum said she had told her that Grandad was dead, and had been for the last six years, but he probably went to his allotment or down the street to the bookies. Gran seemed pleased with this explanation.

Later that afternoon I tried to download more music on to my MP3 player, but after two wasted hours I gave up. I don't know what my husband was thinking of when he bought it for me for my birthday - he knows I'm a complete technophobe. Sarah had at least talked me through downloading Robbie Williams whilst on the phone, trouble is now I have all his songs four times and that is a bit much even for me, not to mention an enormous phone bill. Anyway, I resisted the urge to throw it out of the window. I will buy Terry a cake decorating set for his birthday that will show him.

11th December

Terry is once again installed in his cinema chasing aliens through hyperspace at warp speed; so I phoned Sarah. She had put her Christmas decorations up and informed me that even Jimi Hendrix had tinsel on him. She told me that she had intended to make her boyfriend pancakes for his birthday breakfast, but forgot to buy the eggs so they had toast instead. She promised she would take some photos of her flat to show everyone at Christmas, but would need to have a tidy up first. She also asked if I really wanted the SingStar Take That game as my main gift, saying she knew I was a real technophobe. I retorted that I didn't know what she meant, and said yes, I would love it.

13th December

Ashley sold his X-Box today, got a good price for it although, when left alone, the buyer tried to knock the price down, but Ash held his own and got the agreed price. The purchasers were a strange couple, said they saw a pheasant on the way here which had been clipped by a car, so they got out and kicked it in the head and put it in their boot. Said they did the same with a rabbit last week, although when they cooked it, it didn't taste nice. This, however, had not put them off and they would be stocking up their freezer on road-kill. They kept going on about builders going bust and did we have enough work? I felt like telling them to mind their own business, but my husband said I had to be polite, especially as they asked for some of his business cards, (probably to use them as labels for their freezer).

17

The ex-pats are all a bit like that over here, it seems to attract that sort - loads of money (or did have) and are now living in half-renovated barns kitted out thanks to B&Q. They love to tell you how much money they had back in the UK, what high-powered jobs they did and especially how much they sold their houses for.

"Now we live off the land and eat road kill." I ask you...

However, we are all pretty much the same; fresh off the boat with bucket-loads of cash. We then spend the next two and a half years of our waking lives renovating our derelict, French bargains and eventually running out of money and energy, returning to the U.K crestfallen and bankrupt. It's only a small percentage that sticks it out. You are lucky if you have a guaranteed income and are able to afford to refill your central heating oil tank or purchase vast amounts of seasoned timber to feed your greedy wood burner.

Then, there are the mad ones like us; scratching a living and eking out our central heating oil. Sometimes, even having to resort to burning the wooden pallets that our endless building supplies arrive on.

16th December

Had a busy day and before picking Ashley up from school, called into my favourite shop. It is called "Noz" - it literally means to have a nose about, it's a giant warehouse that sells end of line and bankrupt stock - everything from wine to cotton wool, everything you could ever need and a lot of stuff that you never would.

Put my feet up with the remains of a five litre wine box to watch TV. Did you know if you take the insides out of the box it looks just like a colostomy bag?

Jamie Oliver was on TV. I love the Christmas cookery specials; it does however leave me feeling slightly inadequate. I mean, who has the energy to make Kedgeree for Boxing Day breakfast when most of the real world is still trying to scrape baked-on fat off the roasting dish? It is just not going to happen, he would be better off showing you how to put two Alka-Seltzer in a glass of water, now that would be useful...

As for the smell, you've just spent two weeks trying to get the house to smell all Christmassy, with scented candles and pot-pourri, then bang, gone in an instant. When the neighbours come to exchange Christmas greetings your house smells of Billingsgate fish market. What on earth would my French neighbours think of that? I don't know why I bother watching it; I just end up all tense and then my husband chirps up, "Why don't you make your own Christmas pudding?"

I reply that the local supermarket has started to sell English products, so it would be rude not to buy them now that they are making the effort for us Brits.

17th December

Things to do:

Find the missing balls from the tree (has the dog eaten them?)

Post last Christmas cards

Ashley has gone on a school trip to London. These French teachers are not stupid - it is supposed to be educational, but I think it is just a good way to get paid whilst doing your shopping. Let's face it where do you go Christmas shopping in rural France, and what the hell do they buy?

18th December

Woke up to snow, this is not a good start. Walked the dog and tried not to lose him before taking him to the kennels, or jail as we fondly call it. He wasn't keen, but we coaxed him in.

After leaving contact numbers and explaining that if he did manage to run away we would understand and would not sue them. We made a quick pit stop at the neighbours, Bruno and Odile's, not sure what they made of the Christmas pudding I presented them with.

Odile was in the middle of wrestling a giant sized cockerel over her gas hob, explaining it was the only way to get the bird 'prêt pour le cuisine'. The smell of burning flesh and feathers was worse than any kedgeree.

"Waste of a good pudding," Terry chirped up as we were leaving, "that will end up in their bin. I don't know why you bothered, you know they think the English can't cook," he moaned.

He had a point. Ashley had taken a batch of my homemade mince pies into school the first year we were here. He came home with the tin still full. It turned out no one was that adventurous, all preferring the cellophane wrapped shop bought Madeleines their mothers had provided. Most upset he said they had thought he was trying to poison them, and had all laughed at his dead fly cakes.

We eventually made it through the blizzards to my Mum's and it was a good job we did, as the following day all travel services were suspended. We didn't care, we had arrived and Leicester was alive with Christmas shoppers.

December 22nd

Things to do:

Post last of Christmas cards today or it will be too late and I will end up saving them till next year.... AGAIN!

Visited my Gran, in her care home. She looked well and rested and even recognized me. We had a nice chat and a couple of glasses of Sherry, but she wasn't sure who the man with me was.

"Is this your new husband?" she said, eying him with suspicion.

I explained it was the same old one and we had been married for ten years.

"Oh I thought you had a new one," she chuckled.

"Crikey, Gran, I have had three and that's enough for anyone, I shan't be having anymore."

She told me about Grandad and how he just ignores her. She said she was fed up with him not talking to her, and could I have a word with him to find out what the bloody hell he was playing at. I could hardly say he was playing at being dead could I? So I promised I would do my best.

Poor Gran, she has not been the same since her fall. She insisted on staying in her own home for as long as she could and who could blame her? Then, after many years of driving my Mum mad and running her ragged, she had a fall and ended up in a care home. She hated it and refused to get out of bed, insisting she was not old and no way was she spending her days with the loonies and dribblers who resided in these places. So that was that, she had a private room and, with her special mattress to ensure she didn't get bedsores, she didn't move.

With my Mum, uncles and aunts all visiting, she had her fair share of company and everybody smuggled in goodies and treats for her. Her favourites were pineapple fritters, cream doughnuts, sponge fancies and anything with chocolate near it or on it. She was well looked after and wanted for nothing. The carers had taken to manicuring and painting her nails but, as she told me, it was no life and she wished she wasn't there. So with my deceased Grandad playing her up as well, she really felt she had her hands full.

Christmas Eve, December 24th

Things to do:

POST CHRISTMAS CARDS!!!!!

Ashley and Sarah arrived; all excited, just as Dad was washing-up the breakfast pots.

"Ey up mi duck, the kids have turned up," he shouted excitedly.

"You're early," I exclaimed, hugging them both.

"Yeah, Gran said you were going off to Leicester Christmas shopping early this morning. You wouldn't want me to miss that, would you Mum?" Sarah grinned.

Everyone was looking forward to what Santa would bring, although Ashley had a pretty good idea as a six foot long parcel lay on my Mum's bedroom floor - he had chosen a projector screen off of amazon.com.

Surprisingly it wasn't that busy in Leicester, so we managed to get round and enjoy our shopping. We stopped off at the market to join in the shouting - Sarah is always amazed at the way they sell their wares, saying it was like something from Oliver. She loves joining in with the raucous cries of 'two pounds o'spuds a pound' and 'four caulies three quid'.

It was lovely to be back in Leicester, it was a thrill to see people! The locals are all so friendly and we always seem to bump into someone I am related to. It was all, 'ey up me duck, how's France? Can you speak French yet?'

As most of the villagers worked, or had worked, in the hosiery, engineering or boot and shoe factories, these inquiries were usually shouted at you from across the street, as after years of working along side noisy machinery, most of the village was now deaf. This could be a bit off putting to visitors, but they soon realized the locals are a friendly bunch, they just like to be kept up to date with the goings on of the outside world and quickly learnt not to take any notice of the shouting.

Sarah left after we got home, as she wanted to avoid the traffic and get back before it got dark - she is spending Christmas with her boyfriend at home in Notting Hill, I will miss her. It is never the same without the children and, as much as I pretend I enjoy the peace and rest, the truth is that it is bloody awful. The worst part of divorce is sharing special times. The children, however, have got used to it, even relishing the fact they get two Christmases and loads more presents from their extended family. It has taken me a lot longer to come to terms with it, and that first Christmas nearly broke my heart.

Not wanting to dwell on Sarah's leaving I decided to get ahead with the Christmas dinner, so my Mum's kitchen looks like a bomb has hit it. This is one of the best times to be preparing food - I love this bit, making all the year's preparations come to fruition, decorating everything with sparkly bits. I feel a real "Nigella" moment coming on.

Sarah had bought me some edible glitter off the Internet, so everything will sparkle - even the brussel spouts, well they will if I get my way. Just need to slip into my low cut apron and apply the lippy and you would think you were in the presence of a domestic goddess.

When I was little I would fantasise about being a TV cook. I would bake fairy cakes (cup cakes had not been invented yet) and biscuits, whilst describing how to do it to an imaginary camera. All glamorous, with lots of hand gestures and pouting - very Fanny Craddock. I had seen her on the telly and loved her, her exuberance and style were second to none and I would practice my Fanny impersonations for hours.

A few years ago we were having dinner with friends (Terry had built them a lovely fireplace) and they introduced us to their daughter and her husband. It turned out he was a TV producer.

"Are you telly people?" he enquired.

I told him that neither of us worked in 'telly' but certainly watched enough of it.

He had just finished a series for a TV cook - apparently she wore a wig and had a drink problem. He said she had been a nightmare to work with and, instead of the crew feasting on the fruit of her labours, she would send out for sandwiches from Marks and Spencer's for them. He even hinted that he thought she might not actually be able to cook at all.

Anyway, he had decided he would not do it again, preferring to make programmes about orangutans in Borneo, as he felt they were much less demanding than the primadonna stars of the kitchen. As he so succinctly put it, "She is only a glorified cookery writer. The way she carried on, you would think she was Julia Childs, and there is no way I will ever work with that trumped-up, wig-wearing alcoholic again."

She must have really upset him.

It shattered my illusion of the TV cooks. I thought they were wholly professional and got it right all the time. I had idolized Fanny and her Johnny - in fact I still, to this day, following her recipe for cooking my Christmas turkey, making sure to get right under the skin of the bird and rubbing vast amounts of butter into its' breast.

I sort of wish I hadn't heard the story as it has taken the magic out of it for me, a bit like finding out the tooth fairy doesn't exist. I shall carry on watching though, but perhaps I might just give that particular sloshed, old cook a wide berth for now. Thank goodness there is no dirt on Nigella, she truly is a saint of the kitchen. I think Fanny would have liked her style.

We have been celebrating Christmas with my Mum and Dad for years now, mind you, after the first one we spent with them I thought it might be the last.

It was about fourteen years ago that Terry and I were to spend our first Christmas together. The children had gone to their father's - the dreaded divorce meant sharing them. Terry and I therefore decided to visit my parents.

We went to the local pub and, at the time, my Mum and Dad's friends ran it so everyone knew everyone, except Terry - he was new to it all. There was a fantastic atmosphere and we all got very merry, including my Mum and Dad. We managed to stagger back to my parent's house in the small hours of the morning and all collapsed into bed.

Suddenly, early in the morning, I was rudely awakened by Terry bursting into our bedroom stark naked, having only covered himself for modesty with my Mum's flowery curtains.

"Karen, Karen wake up, something terrible has happened, I think I have just slept with your parents!" he cried.

It seems he had got up in the night being thirsty and needing the loo, but on the way back to our room he got lost and ended up in my Mum and Dad's bed. However, by the time this happened Mum had earlier got up and gone to sleep in the spare room as Dad was snoring his head off. One side of the bed was therefore vacant and Terry had simply slipped under the covers, naked, next to my Dad.

I decided to go downstairs to make a cup of tea and find out what the damage was.

Dad was in the kitchen having a cigarette and reading the News of the World.

"Dad, I think Terry might have slept with you and Mum".

"I know," my Dad said, "I thought it was your Mum, I put my arms around him thinking, ey up me lucks in, she hasn't got her nightie on! Then I realized it was your Terry! Your Mum has a better figure," my Dad sniggered.

No one knew yet what had happened to her. She was oblivious to it all and it turned out that she was safely tucked up asleep in the spare room.

It could have been so much worse! I was so glad Terry was out cold when this had happened and had not responded to my Dad's attentions. Thank God Mum had gone off to sleep in the spare bed.

December 27th

Phoned my friend Julia and wished her a happy Christmas. I explained we would be staying down the road at Annie's for a night before returning to France and wondered if they would be free. She said she wasn't sure as she and Jerry were going to salsa classes every night, but they might just be able to skip one.

"Oh don't put yourself out, we could just meet up for a coffee," I said. Actually, I had rather been hoping for dinner.

She then said she had just been saying to Jerry a couple of days earlier that they must get in touch with us to arrange a visit to France, as we always made them feel so welcome. I made a mental note to be busy the next time they wanted a free holiday in Normandy.

You get this a lot living in a big old farmhouse in the French countryside. Everyone thinks you're always on holiday and open to visitors. I suppose it is our fault having a house called 'Hôtel Marion'. The name gives out the wrong impression.

Don't get me wrong, we love having visitors. It's just that as the house is never finished and we are always in a state of renovation, it becomes a mad dash to finish the latest project, tidy up, shave my legs, pluck my eyebrows and try to look relaxed.

With the bed making, shopping, entertaining and cooking, we feel we are the ones in need of a holiday when the visitors depart. In fact, with all the food, wine and electricity our visitors consume, it would be cheaper for us to go en vacances.

We live in France, but only eat croissants when we have guests and I feel I have to buy them fresh from the boulangerie.

No wonder people want to come and stay - I really must work on becoming less hospitable. However, the truth of the matter is that you get so fed up and lonely here that any visitor is a distraction from the mundaneness of living in the middle of a field.

That is how we became friends with the Jehovah Witnesses. Imagine, day after day, the same old routine, cleaning, walking the dog, popping into Noz, surfing the net, checking Facebook, then out of the blue, a visitor arrives on your door step! We invite them in, desperate for conversation and a break in routine, truly heaven sent!

No wonder Colin and his merry band of Jehovah's Witnesses have such an easy time getting to talk to people in Normandy, let's face it the ex-pats living here have got bugger all else to do.

They go round with French Jehovah's witnesses too and one of them told me they couldn't believe how friendly the English are to them. They are always being invited in and are always up for a cup of tea and a chat.

Anyway, back to the visitors, there are a few exceptions – Annie, my Mum, Dad and Sarah don't count. They just muck in. Annie, my Mum and Dad are far more relaxing to have around, although I do still feel the need to try and get everything perfect for my Mum's arrival - I sometimes still feel like a child, seeking her approval.

Annie likes to cook and is quite happy to take over the kitchen, but we do have to search the shelves of the biggest supermarkets to try and locate the bizarre array of ingredients and spices, so readily available in the UK, that are needed for her culinary extravaganzas. These strange, unheard of ingredients cost a fortune and will sit gathering dust in the pantry until her next visit, but she does knock up some good nosh. I wonder if she fantasised about being a famous TV chef, or was it just me? I will make a note to ask her.

My Mum loves to clean out my cupboards and rearrange my pantry, it has become quite a joke with us. Last time she came to visit we had a sweepstake on how long it would take before she gave in her to her irresistible urge to tidy up. Ashley won with a bet of two hours and twenty-five minutes, not bad.

Anyway, if Julia and Jerry are too busy doing the tango to see us we will settle for a curry and a night in with Annie, surfing the Internet looking for hot men (for her, not me, well not much).

December 29th

Things to do:

Unpack

Put un-posted Christmas cards away for next year

Hide my brother's tin of Quality Street so I don't eat them and the rest of the goodies my Mum has sent him

Looking forward to relaxing in a warm bath, putting my pyjamas on and letting it all hang out by not wearing my bra. I can't do this in polite company, as there is always the risk I will take someone's eye out or frighten small children. So, to go bra-less and have a good old scratch is my kind of heaven, I think my husband was planning a similar version involving his dangly bits, but didn't like to ask.

Glad to be back home and sleeping in my own bed again. It has been very wearing sharing a queen sized bed with my husband snoring his head off all night and, with my Dad doing the same in the next room, I felt like jumping out of bed and conducting their not so orchestral sounds. Luckily the girl in the next-door house was usually having sex at the same time, so I had something to take my mind off it. I think I would have gone mad otherwise.

Picked Sam, the dog, up from the kennels, unfortunately he had not run away and I was informed that he had, in fact, been one of their better-behaved dogs. All I can say is that there must be some very badly behaved hounds out there. Let's see if his spell in jail has cured him of his thievery and running away or if he was just hoping for early release for good behaviour.

New Year, New Me, or Same Old Dog?

January 4th

Welcome to a new year. I hate New Year's Eve, as it always seems like you must have a good time and usually it falls flat on its face for me. We did have a fun time playing Sing Star in Ashley's bedroom, (too cold in the cinema). His French girlfriend really thinks we are crazy English now, if only she was not too shy to speak I am sure she would say so.

Well this is it a new beginning - I can now open my heart to my diary. It may only be paper and my pen but at least I have something to confide in. It is starting to help – even I can see that. Could my diary be responsible for my lighter mood – had I found a way to survive this loneliness? Even Terry had commented on my change in demeanour.

I just have to carry on writing it and, believe me, there are always a thousand other things to do. Days just fill themselves with trivia, I mean, I have to check my e-mails, have a look on Facebook so I can see what my daughter has been up to. It's like a modern espionage service. I feel obliged to read the free ads on the expat's forum 'Anglais Rural Society for Ex-pats' or, as I like to call it 'ARSE', to see what returning Brits are selling off cheap.

So by the time I've walked the dog and done the cleaning, listened to my mum moaning about the antics of my Dad, it's another day over. Like an alcoholic taking the pledge, I promised myself I would continue to write, even if I found it hard.

I was born in a little village in Leicestershire, surrounded by fields and family. A lot of famous people come from Leicester, including the Attenborough boys, Englebert Humperdinck, Gok Wan and Sue Townsend, who created my personal hero, Adrian Mole. During the seventies I attended the village infants' school and was part of an experiment that was carried out by the County. Known as ITA, it was a way of learning how to read and spell phonetically - you know, KAT for cat etc. Anyway, it really messed me up and I have spent the rest of my life trying to undo the damage it caused me and learn to spell correctly. I'm sure you could sue them today for damages.

Anyway, I was enjoying writing my journal, I had more time on my hands than the lifers incarcerated at Her Majesty's pleasure, if not the grammar and punctuation and spelling skills. What was spell check for anyway? Surely it was invented for illiterate types like me? I think I might actually be Dyslexic (or is it dicslecsic?), but we didn't have words like that when I was growing up. When I asked my Mum, she said she thought I was just a bit slow.

Put up my new Robbie Williams calendar; how long will it be before he has a moustache and a fake beard drawn all over him? Ashley asked if I had noticed that Robbie was dressed as a rabbit in the April picture.

"Pull the other one." I replied.

Slightly peeved that I had not believed him he showed Terry and asked for his confirmation. I finally went over to have a look and, there on the April page, he really was dressed as a rabbit complete with bunny ears.

"Hmm, I see what you mean." I said, not wanting to show the shock in my voice, (it really was all a bit strange).

"It's not the official calendar" I quickly retorted, defending Robbie. I didn't think even he would have agreed to use a photo like that.

"Sarah told me that she couldn't buy the official calendar off the Internet, so I don't suppose he had much say in the photos," I rather lamely offered up.

Ashley just sniggered and said "still a bit gay though Mum, don't you think?"

January 11th

Well, hibernation mode has really settled in. It's so boring here in the winter with nowhere to go and there really is nothing to do. So I dug out some DVD's from Terry's cinema. At this time of the year I really like a good disaster film; plane crashes, train crashes, car crashes, any kind of crash really. My personal favourite is one about a plane crash in the snowy mountains, where the survivors have to eat each other - that really cheers me up.

I got the wood in, stoked up the fires and prepared to wake up in March. Decided to open my brother's tin of Quality Street - in my defence they were giving me the eye and Ashley encouraged me. It might be a while before we see him, so I had plenty of time to buy some more, I assured myself, before tucking in.

Work is always quiet for Terry and the rest of the building trade at this time of the year. Nobody has any money left after Christmas for continuing with the renovation of their homes and, even if they do, they prefer to have their new windows fitted when it is somewhat warmer.

Terry had just got home from his last job of this month, so we may have a cold and meagre start to the New Year – again! He had warned me to stock up the pantry and get out there chopping wood. So, if we live frugally we should just about hole up through the worst of it, and if the worst comes to the worse there's always the road kill!

Terry was in good spirits and was bursting to relay the events of his day. He had been working for Tina and Elaina, the Dutch lesbians, who were new to the area. Terry's job was to support the bedroom floor as it was sagging in the middle – I joked about him being able to do plastic surgery, but he just ignored me, preferring to carry on telling his tale with gusto.

He had turned up not knowing exactly what was required. Sometimes people hire him for a day to do all of the carpentry jobs they cannot manage themselves. He was therefore a little bemused when the first thing Tina asked him to do was to help her move a dead alpaca. He helped her to carry it onto a pre-prepared table in the barn so that she could perform an autopsy. Luckily, he explained, he was not required to gown-up and assist further and was able to carry on with his more usual work.

To his relief he later learned, over coffee, that Tina had been a vet in Holland and as the alpaca had died suddenly the previous evening, she had decided to carry out an autopsy to ascertain the cause of death. What seemed to annoy her even more, she explained, was that she had not got round to milking the alpaca before its demise and was now short of milk.

This meant that they had to put up with goat's milk in their tea instead. I made a mental note that if he worked for them again I would make him up a thermos!

Eventually I was able to ask him the burning question on which I had been pondering ever since I had heard Elaina's husky and rather sexy voice on the telephone.

"So," I enquired, "what are they like, are they attractive?"

He thought so, as long as you like the Fatima Whitbread look. Tina was all muscle and sported a blonde, close-cropped hairstyle, whilst Elaina was extremely well endowed and did not seem to wear a bra. Although fascinated, he did not know where to look whilst drinking his goat's milk laden tea. He said it was like watching two large ferrets trying to escape from a sack. I shook my head in despair as I started to make the dinner.

January 12th

Woke up to snow! Loads of snow, snow as far as you can see. It looked so amazing that suddenly the hibernation was put on hold and the desire to run wildly through crisp snow gripped us all. Sam loved it; he had his own way of making snow angels and couldn't get enough of it, rolling in it, snuffling it, eating it and, of course, pooing in it.

Madness descended upon me. I decided to let him off the lead to run free. Everywhere looked so beautifully clean and fresh and I just wanted him to experience the thrill of being let off the lead and running through virgin snow. Big mistake, he took one look at me and bolted.

After shouting myself hoarse I realised that he was not coming back. Never mind, it was only 3.00pm and still light, he would be back soon I reassured myself and went home and put the kettle on. He had run off many times, but always came back eventually; filthy, stinking of something in explainable, exhausted and hungry with that familiar hang-dog look that said 'I know I am bad, but I just can't help myself'. He would then proceed to slink over to his bed, putting himself in the doghouse for the night, refusing to make any eye contact.

4.00pm - Still no sign of him and now it's starting to get dark, so I go out armed with the fireworks that we use to get him to come back. The use of these little bangers might sound a bit cruel, but the explosive retort would always make him run for home. No luck, no sign and I'm starting to get worried.

5.30pm - All been out looking for Sam, no barking, no footprints. He has really gone this time. It was blowing a gale and it had started to snow heavily again. We were all worried sick about him, how the hell could he survive a night out in these conditions? I could feel tears pricking at my eyelids because, despite the fact that I often felt like killing him, I really loved my emotionally deranged pet and now could not imagine life without him.

6.30 pm – The phone rang and Ashley rushed to answer it. It was an elderly French lady explaining in a strong patois that she had phoned Bruno, our neighbour, to find out if he knew who owned a golden retriever who was currently sitting in her kitchen being fed pâté and cheese. She told us where she lived and that we could pick him up in the morning because of the bad weather. I said we would go immediately as I was afraid that if he stayed any longer we would have a bill for new cushions, bathmats, socks and shoes.

January 20th

This is a bad time of year for me as it is the anniversary of my son Matthew's death. From year to year I handle it differently. This year I felt I was holding it together pretty well - I think the dog had a lot to do with it.

Last April my son would have been twenty-one years old and it had been tough. It was tough enough without being asked almost daily by my well-meaning Mum if I was going to England to put flowers on his grave. Yes, I suppose I should go, but I just wanted to forget it. I know that sounds harsh, but I had had enough of being strong for so many years; always putting on a brave face, having to carry on when inside I felt like curling up and dying. I didn't want to cry, I didn't want to dissolve into depression. I didn't want to, but I had, and I was behaving quite badly. Instead of letting it out I was keeping it in; I was afraid if I started to cry I would never stop.

Every January one day will emerge from the frozen, wintery bleakness as a promise of things to come. A tantalising glimpse of better things just waiting around the corner – a promise that spring is creeping up on us and pushing its way through the cold, cruel earth.

January 21st 1990 was one of those days. We had awoken to sunshine streaming through the closed curtains, tempting us to go outside. I was delighted to escape into the garden after being imprisoned in the house with a two and three-quarter-year-old toddler and Sarah, who was eighteen-months old. After a long search, Matthew's wellington-boots were found and an array of hats and scarves had to be displayed for Sarah to make her choice of outdoor wear for the day. With a little effort, the rusty old padlock securing the shed was unlocked and an array of toys and garden tools were quickly strewn across the leaf-carpeted patio.

The children were so thrilled to re-discover the joys of their sandpit, which had lain dormant all winter under a blanket of leaves. I was busy sweeping and collecting the winter debris and as we filled our lungs with fresh warm air, soon the scarves, hats and coats were discarded in the unexpected and magical January sunshine.

After a morning's hard work and play I went indoors to collect drinks and snacks for a well-deserved picnic lunch. Matthew and Sarah followed me inside and I gave them the crusts from the sandwiches I was making and told them to feed the ducks, which were all gathered hungrily on the wooden jetty protruding into the backwater of the Thames beside which our house lay. She returned quickly without the bread so I gave her the remaining crusts to do the same again.

I then suddenly realised that she was alone. I was not worried at that point because, with a secure fence enclosing our garden, I knew no harm could come to the children. However, I still not like to leave them in the garden alone without me. I had left them unattended for more than a few minutes and that is sometimes all that it takes. I ran outside, but Matthew was nowhere to be found with a quick scan of the garden and the shed.

I then turned my attention to inside the house and, on searching, still could not find him. He was not hiding under his bed; he was nowhere to be seen. At eighteen months, Sarah did not speak very clearly so was not able to give me any clues as to his whereabouts.

Screaming and calling out his name did not yield anything and I frantically telephoned my neighbour and friend, Christine, whilst checking everywhere again. She came straight round and we searched all of the obvious places again and, finally, the river – but still nothing, he had disappeared and was nowhere to be seen.

We both agreed that it was time to call the police. Christine started knocking on neighbouring doors. We wondered if he had managed get through into the front garden and wandered off up the lane to see the ponies. She reassured me that he could not have got into the water as there was a secure fence all around the garden – how could a toddler of Matthew's age have got over or through it? We continued to search, with the neighbours joining in and one of them decided to take out her little red rowing boat and check the river.

Venturing down the river she found his little body, he was unconscious and face down floating in the water. Being a nurse, she knew what to do and at the same time the ambulance and police arrived. It seemed like it was all happening at once. They all tried to resuscitate him, without success, and he was taken in an ambulance to the local hospital with me following behind in a police car.

I had telephoned my husband as soon as I had contacted the police when we realised that Matthew really was missing. He had rushed home and met the ambulance at the end of the road and travelled with them to the hospital.

Nobody could have tried harder to save him. He was in Accident and Emergency for five hours and it was explained to us that there was a slight possibility that they could save his life. His blood was taken from his small body, now almost blue with cold, and put through a machine to warm it and then returned once it had reached a certain temperature.

They were then able to use a defibrillator to try to restart his heart. The Consultant explained that he had successfully done this before with another little boy who had fallen into a river. It did not happen; he did not warm up enough and was pronounced dead. I sat holding his hand willing him to live, but it was fruitless.

We had lost him – our beautiful, mischievous little boy was no longer with us. I thought my heart would burst with the pain I felt. The ache was unbearable; I had lost my first-born child – my funny, beautiful little lad. I had left him alone for just a few minutes. I knew it was all my fault and that my life would never be the same again. I had let him down and not been there for him when he needed me most. I had lost him and lost some of me that day. I am not the same any more – everything changed.

Coping is a mechanism we all use - some successfully, where others just flounder around in grief forever. I am a fighter and had to be strong; after all I had Sarah and had to carry on her for her. I had lost one child, but she still needed me.

You see, it was not that simple; Matthew died accidentally down at the bottom of our own garden whilst in my care. That was bad enough for anyone to live with, but there was more to it than that.

Matthew had stormed into our lives on Easter Sunday 1988, larger than life and looking and weighing the same as a three month old baby. He would pull himself up in his cot and the nurses would comment that he looked like he had been here before.

Loving and affectionate he carried on growing and, demandingly, took over our lives. He terrorised everybody at the Mother and Toddler Group and I was told in no uncertain terms that he was 'trouble'. He would push over babies and launch himself over anything in his way. He certainly was a handful.

Everything needed to be taken out of his reach; on one occasion he had thrown a whole drawer-full of Sarah's clothes into the river and been thoroughly scolded for it. He had removed an electric plug with a plastic screwdriver that his Grandad had given him, so this had to be confiscated. He constantly woke in the night and was hungry all the time. He simply exhausted me.

I was run ragged. I hardly slept or ate and never had five minutes to myself. So, when he died I was, that first night, strangely relieved as I thought my life would be much easier now. I felt I had wished him dead. It was my entire fault he had died. How could any mother live with these thoughts? I hated myself.

Well-meaning friends and family tried to comfort me by saying it was not my fault and that it could happen to anyone, but I felt in my heart that I had made it happen. Wishing him away and wanting peace and quiet, thinking sometimes that life would be easier without children. I was an evil mother. I would spend the rest of my life torturing myself with the guilt and grief of these thoughts.

If only I had stopped him. If only I had not taken my eye off him. I had no idea that night of the magnitude of the pain that would follow and the loss and emptiness. He had been the centre of our world, cramming everything into his short life and even twenty years later I still ache for him, ache to hold him and ache to have known him – my beautiful Matthew.

All those years later the pain was still with me and I was reliving that day and the subsequent week with the morbid clarity that grief brings to you. I was torturing myself, struggling along with the weight of my misery, which was pulling me further and further down.

Then twenty years later, on the anniversary of Matthews's death, a strange thing happened.

Terry came home with a dog. Sam was a five-year old golden retriever belonging to some German clients and they had to find a new home for him. He was with us for a week on trial as Wolfgang, his owner, was going back to Germany at the weekend and if it didn't work out then Sam would go back with him.

I was ecstatic, I had always wanted a dog and this one was so handsome. In fact, rather spookily, I noticed that we even had similar hairstyles. He, along with a bitch called Jenny, had been part of a breeding pair. Between them they had produced two litters, so they now needed to find a new home for Sam. Wolfgang's wife had got a new job as an estate agent and Sam needed to be around people, he didn't like being left on his own. Apparently Jenny was fine, but they said that Sam was a big softy who just loved company and attention. Anyway, this is the story they told us.

I fell in love with Sam. He wooed me with his soppy eyes, his peaceful manner and his obedience - he was a perfect dog. Wolfgang went back to Germany with Jenny and I soon learnt that Sam had conned me.

The second week I found out why people give dogs away. Before leaving Wolfgang had given us a list:

Do not let him off the lead, he will run away

No bones, they are bad for him

He hates thunderstorms, gunshots, loud bangs, fireworks

He does not like towns and traffic

He likes water

He loves to go out in the car

He's not very good with cats

He loves other dogs

He doesn't like the vet

Don't touch his bottom - he hates it and will growl at you (why would I want to, or indeed need to?)

You must walk him three times a day, as he doesn't do his business in the garden

Don't leave him too long on his own, as he gets lonely (ahh, sweet)

How hard could it be? He was just a dog.

I soon found out it could be really hard; just the three walks a day had given me blisters and the dog seemed knackered. However, this did not deter him from stealing my soft furnishings and having a special fondness for cushions, bathmats, socks and shoes.

All doors had to remain closed, as nothing was sacred. We found we had to do this after he had eaten two pairs of my glasses, three slippers, a decorative ornament, a paper maché hedgehog, a cigarette lighter, a packet of toilet rolls, part of the Hoover and countless socks.

So, I gave in and bought him a bone.

He did, however, take my mind off my sorrow and I was too busy to cry, but you never forget.

Hard Times and Alcohol

1st February

Annie is coming to visit. We can go shopping and have lunch and I will have someone to watch X Factor with on Saturday night. Terry can't stand it and says they are all rubbish, I think he's just jealous because he thinks he's so much better than the contestants but is too scared to audition.

Annie and I had the same circle of friends, we were close, but certainly not best friends. She had been there when Matthew died, but everyone had been there for me, the whole village mourned with us. So, when I moved to North Devon it came as a surprise when she phoned me, out of the blue.

"What's the news from your neck of the woods?" I asked.

"Oh, Tony has left me, gone off with some slapper with big knockers and a fat arse," she said.

"How strange," I replied, "as mine has gone off with a skinny bird with pert tits and a pierced belly button!"

Isn't it funny how opposites attract? I was on the rounder side, my stomach had stopped being exposed a long time ago and my boobs were on a downward slide, while Annie was a slim size ten all over, (lucky bitch).

"I expect they fancied a change." I said

So, from that day on we were allies, crying together, laughing together but mainly drinking together.

After a few months we were fed up with feeling like rejects and putting up with all the rubbish that kicking out your husband involves.

While our ex's were off, presumably having fabulous sex and in the first throes of a new romance, we were stuck at home working and trying to bring up the children, who thought it was all our fault their Daddy had gone.

It is so difficult trying to explain to small children that you threw their beloved Father out because he was having sex with another woman - they just don't get it.

Life is sometimes shit.

Between us, we decided what we needed was a break, get away from it all and have a week in Greece. We were sure that this would sort us out, and a package trip was duly booked.

We had to wait until half term, however, as we had no one to look after the kids. Ex-husbands can sometimes come in handy, but not very often.

You know it's going to be a good holiday when you start drinking vodka at six am.

It didn't disappoint.

It was the coldest, wettest holiday I have ever been on, we had two days of warm weather and then the heavens opened, but we didn't notice.

The first night we thought we would take it easy, yeah right... after the vodka for breakfast the tone had been set.

Inside the gaudily decorated Karaoke bar, it was heaving and despite an abysmal performance from the man in the anorak, who was crucifying 'Hey Jude' with his monotone rendition, no one seemed to bother. In fact, next up was 'Honeley tha lohneley' which was only a slight improvement.

"Por favour, s'il vous plait, mon amigo," I screeched over the drone of the hapless chap.

I figured that as I didn't speak Greek, then a mixture of Spanish and French was the next best thing.

The dark haired, swarthy looking barman bellowed, "Yeah love what d'ya want? Sex on the beach? Or a long comfortable screw?"

"Oh you're English, then?" I asked ignoring his innuendo.

"Luton, love, now what d'ya fancy?"

"Well actually could you do me and my mate a big favour and pretend were old friends? That creepy Greek guy has followed us from the Santorini Shish Kebab shop up the road."

"Oh the waiter from hell, he's a well-known stalker of fresh meat, a bloody nutcase, yeah, you do right, keep well away from that loony lothario!"

Before I realized what was happening and able to protest (yeah right), I had been grabbed by the barman in a rough embrace and he was snogging my face off, (and I was quite enjoying it) as I surfaced I could see our pursuer thankfully exiting the bar. It had worked.

"Might as well do a proper job, always keen to help out." The barman smugly explained

"Do you two know each other?" Annie inquired.

"We do now." I sniggered, winking at her.

Now asking for help in this way indeed turned out to be the best chat-up line you could ever think of and resulted in us being the centre of attention with all the staff. We were given free shots as we worked our way through the cocktails presented; we also seemed to be getting more money back than we were paying out. We were certainly not going to complain, as after all this was the attention we had come for.

It wasn't long before we were up on stage singing our socks off, giving it everything we had, (which in all fairness wasn't much).

Annie did a couple of wonderful solo performances the ultimate of which was her portrayal of the Celine Dion classic, 'All by myself.' Complete with tears and mascara running down her pained face. Finally and dramatically, she dropped to the floor arms outstretched in an imploring manner, somehow managing not to fall out of her sequined boob tube. Her finale was a triumph. They loved her!

The room erupted with shouts and clapping, she was a star. This had seemed to do the trick, and there were a number of takers to make sure she wasn't going to spend the night all by herself.

Rounding the night of, we both jumped up on to the stage for a drunken duet of Sister Sledge's 'We are family'.

Now completely smashed and wasted, if it hadn't been for the owner closing the bar we would have still been up there, punishing the ears of any passing tourists.

Our holiday had truly begun.

Annie met a man on our second night, in the same bar. He was staying in our hotel and had heard us come in the evening before.

"So it was you two who made all that racket and dropped the fire extinguisher down the stairs," he said smiling.

We must have impressed him, as the next day he arranged to take Annie off jet skiing.

I was fine with this, as I had teamed up with the barman, who was pining for a girl he had met earlier in the season. I had just started going out with Terry, and although we weren't serious, I behaved myself, (well, as best you can with all that Sun Sea and free flowing cocktails).

Annie and her northern soul had hit it off big time and she was loving it. The only problem being that he was off home before us, so they didn't have much time - but they sure as hell made the most of it.

We had the time of our lives and came back confident, refreshed and very good at karaoke.

2nd February

Mum phoned to say that she had been to see Gran who was up to her old tricks again, not getting out of bed and swearing at her cares. Mum managed to calm her down, which was usually best accomplished with food.

"This makes a welcome change! They are feeding me muck," Gran had complained.

"At this rate I'll be dead in six months, I swear they are starving me to death," she had carried on between munching on her custard tart, and slurping her sherry through a straw.

When we first moved to Normandy we asked our neighbour, Bruno, the farmer, if they ever had snow.

"Non." He informed us shaking his head as he walked away.

Needless to say it has snowed every year since we arrived, and today was looking like an artic blizzard had blown in.

Sam is sleeping after his walk, so I have a few hours before he starts prowling, looking for something to steal and run off with.

A few months after the dog arrived, my husband decided to go against all the rules (this usually happens when he's had a drink), so he let Sam out at midnight, thinking he might need a wee. God knows why he got that idea into his head, as that dog has a cast iron bladder and has been known not to get off his bed until midday and, even then, it takes some persuasion.

Anyway, Terry let him out and it goes without saying that Sam had his wee and bolted. Great - so at two o'clock in the morning, after shouting for him and setting off bangers, the dog had not returned. We decided to go to bed, fearing the worst and thinking this time we had really lost him.

No such luck - at half past four he woke me up, barking outside the front door. Terry was snoring away and oblivious to it all, so I went downstairs to let Sam in and hopefully get back to bed.

He was completely filthy and totally hyper, jumping up at me and covering me, and the whole of the kitchen, in mud and saliva. It was no good; I got his lead, pulled on my wellies and in the freezing cold small hours of the morning, there I was hosing down a mud-caked dog. I cleaned him up, toweled him dry and got him settled in the kitchen, cunningly barricading him in so that he could not run riot over the rest of the house.

As I climbed into bed I thought of Wolfgang, his previous owner, fast asleep in a warm cozy bed in his nice clean house in Germany, safe in the knowledge he had palmed us off with his mad senseless dog.

4th February

The good thing about living in Normandy is that you do not have to take your Christmas decorations down on Twelfth Night, in fact in some communes it is obligatory to keep them up until at least Easter. My mum couldn't believe it when I told her that the butcher in the village still had their Christmas tree up - I said I would e-mail her a photo to prove it.

"Those French, they like to get their money's worth," she tittered.

Ashley telephoned to say that the school had to close because of the snow. It will be mashed potatoes for tea then, as his girlfriend Sophie is coming to stay too. Just hope she has got a coat this time.

Sam, the dog, wasn't the first Sam in my life. I was born in a flat on the high street in a small industrial village in the Midlands and for the first three and half years of my life I tormented most of the people that lived near to us.

I was particularly fond of an old man called Sam. He was so old that I never saw him move. He just sat in his chair sucking on humbugs and taking pinches of snuff, which he smelt of, along with a kind of musty, mothball old peoples' odour and I loved him. I loved everything about him. I would sit on his lap curled up like a cat snuggled up to him, breathing in his being and pinching his sweets sometimes from his mouth. He was just too old to argue and protest.

I just could not be torn away from him and spent many a happy hour in the dimly lit kitchen huddled up with him in his chair by the open fire, whilst watching his daughter, Elsie, going about her chores. She had dedicated her life to looking after him in his old age and, although quite old herself, she had refused to marry and move out preferring to stay at home to look after her old Dad. She had a boyfriend, Arthur, and he would visit sometimes. He wanted to marry her, but she would not leave her beloved dad.

I liked to help Elsie as she was always so busy rushing around. She had a habit of leaving her washing-up bowl full of water when she had finished her pots, so I would assist by emptying it and putting her tea towels away for her. However this was not as helpful as I presumed and she would shout at me for throwing away her hot water and hiding her cloths. I would just jump up on to Sam's lap for protection and we would snigger behind our hands together at her ranting. I must have driven her mad, but I think she put up with me because she was touched that someone else loved her Dad as much as she did.

There was also my uncle and aunt who lived next door. We all had gardens with toilets at the bottom of them, but my uncle Den's was the best, (his garden not his toilet). He was the Alan Titchmarsh of our street and could grow anything. He was a miner and therefore spent most of his day's underground digging for coal. I suppose that is why he loved his garden so much and spent most of his waking hours out there happily tending it, as well as reading cowboy books and drinking beer in his greenhouse.

One particularly hot summer it was left to my mum to tend the garden as my aunt and uncle went off to Skegness for their annual holiday. Ever helpful, I decided I would give my Mum a hand. By now my baby brother had been born and, like Elsie, my Mum seemed to always be rushing about.

Unfortunately my helping hand consisted of ripping up all of the young cabbages out of the ground, thinking they were weeds. My Mum was furious and scared stiff of what his reaction would be on his return, knowing how fastidious he was about his vegetables. She quickly tried to replant them and water them in, but she was fighting a losing battle with the searing heat of that summer not helping one jot. She tried giving them the best chance to grow again, but it seemed like a fruitless mission and I was told in no uncertain terms to leave other peoples things alone and stop trying to be helpful.

On their return my Mum anxiously explained what I had done but he simply smiled and said,

"Ah bless her she was only trying to help".

Soon after this episode we moved house. We had been on the Council waiting list and we had been allocated a three bed roomed semi-detached house with its own fenced-in garden and inside toilet. I think my Mum was happy to know I would be contained in our own garden and no longer able to be out roaming the streets and terrorising our neighbours.

5th February

We had a decent job lined up for April but on checking my e-mails this morning they have cancelled it. Apparently their horse had gone lame, expensive vets bills were expected.

This does happen a lot - you get offered the carrot of good times, money in the bank, fuel for the central heating and that new front door we so desperately need. Then with one e-mail, (it is always e-mails now, it really has made breaking bad news so much easier)

44

your dreams are squashed and it's back to freezing to death and shopping at Aldi.

Tried to broach the subject with Terry we were drowning in debt barley able to hold our heads above water, whilst working our butts off. Something had to change.

"It's the time of the month you always go on like this when you're hormonal." He argued.

"It's not that, I'm fed up with us trying to scratch a living, we rarely go out as we've never got any money, and your always so tired all you want to do is watch Star Trek." I cried.

"Well you were the one who brought us here, you wanted the big house the tranquility a slower pace of life; anyway what am I the entertainments manager? and there is nothing wrong with Star Trek. You should try it might calm you down."

"Well I got it wrong, I've had enough of peace and quiet, and I want my life back." I said, angrily slamming the door as I grabbed the dogs lead.

Walking through the deserted woods with only the sound of leaves crunching under my feet to break the silence, I started to reflect, this wasn't what I wanted, I needed companionship, I needed a friend.

Terry was great he was patient and put up with my moaning and tantrums but it wasn't enough I was not cut out for this isolated lifestyle it was eating me up, and I can't stand Star Trek.

You have to be tough to stick it out here; you have to face the fact that the Normans can't work out where we get our money from - with our flash cars, our big houses and our satellite TV with the BBC on tap.

Mind you, it is not just the foreigners they dislike, the Parisians are something else and, of course, the Parisians think they so much more 'champagne' than 'campagne'.

They believe that anyone who was not born in Paris is a peasant and most probably married to their own cousin. Consequently their fellow countrymen are beneath their contempt.

So, while they have an aversion to their fellow compatriots, they dream of escaping the city and living in the countryside. Hence, this is why so many have migrated to Normandy. Parisians are now being blamed for the inflated house prices, fancy bistros with their exclusive menus. The Parisians are intent on changing the face of rural Normandy. So, you can see why we get on so well with them.

Unsurprisingly the only French friends we do have in Normandy are originally from Paris.

One very cold day about four years ago, we had been working locally and decided to pop home for a warm-up and something to eat. Sitting huddled in the kitchen with our coats still on, there was a knock on the door. It was a travelling wine salesman who introduced himself as Maxim. Terry informed him that he would be most welcome to enter if we could taste his wares.

"Bien sûr" was his reply.

Maxim was why the French invented the word 'suave' - he was Mr Sex Appeal - all testosterone and garlic, dressed immaculately with pointy, crocodile skin shoes.

He was duly invited in and, larger than life and sexier than Sacha Distel, he took over the kitchen table and changed our lives. After consuming copious amounts of wine, we gave him our order and Terry and I went for a lie down.

Maxim, the sexy wine merchant became a regular visitor, mainly because he surmised that as we were English we could not resist a free glass of wine. This enabled him to gain an order a sober man would never have placed.

So we became friends; his wife, Jacqueline came to visit and she was even more chic than Maxim. With her designer handbags, manicured nails and taunting cleavage, she was certainly very different to the Normandy housewives I was used to bumping into at Marche U, who favoured their floral polyester overalls, pop-socks and Crocs.

Maxim and Jacqueline would often bring their son, Flavian when they visited and then, one day, finally we met Basile, Maxim's papa. It was immediately apparent where Maxim got his style from. Basile was always in tight fitting white jeans, cowboy boots, silk shirt and a leather jacket. He looked a bit like Richard Fairbrass, you know the bald guy from the group Right Said Fred. He was charismatic, always up for a laugh and incredibly good at jiving.

We were in. We had friends at last!

We were invited to family parties and soirées, thus meeting the whole entourage, brothers, sisters, aunts, and uncles. On one occasion Maxim nearly fell off his chair when I asked if Basile was gay, as I had never heard mention of Maxims mum and Basile did sport a certain style.

"No Kaarren," Maxim assured me, "he just adores Johnny Hallyday and likes to mimic his style. My Mama ran off with a travelling sock sales man when I was an énfant."

After several of these drunken buying sessions we had the bright idea of inviting all our friends and customers to have our own giant wine tasting. It would be like a party, but we wouldn't have to buy the booze!

This turned out to be an excellent idea and over the years we've had our fair share of free parties.

Mind you, when I say free it doesn't usually work out that way. Terry, who enjoys a good drink at the best of times, excels at these wine-tasting soirées. The last one left us with an order of over six hundred euros worth of alcohol. I'm not sure if he was showing off or if he got over excited at the thought of all that booze.

Words were exchanged over the large cheque presented to Maxim, as we didn't even have enough money to pay for the central heating oil. As long as we stayed two sheets to the wind we wouldn't notice that we were freezing to death, he did spend a lot of time sloping of to his cinema until I had calmed down.

Maxim was not only a wine salesman but also a D.J - he had the lot; flashing lights, turntables, karaoke. He really was Monsieur Entertainment and he would bring all his gear and party on down. So on one of these occasions he had finished selling wine for the day and switched to his alter-ego. Donning a gold lamé jacket and, unbuttoning his shirt, he launched himself onto the dance floor.

Our dining room now resembled a seedy nightclub in Faliraki. With the first beats of Motorhead's Ace of Spades, he was in the middle of the floor air-guitaring with the best of them.

With little entertainment on offer in rural Normandy, all we had on the social calendar was the Meschui with the ancient combatants and an evening of Belote with the Société de Chasse. Everyone was making the most of it, knowing that a barbequed sheep and a game of cards weren't much to look forward to.

Although, I was sad to see Odile (Bruno the farmer's wife) leaving early, Bruno explained that someone had to milk the cows. Arms and legs were flying with the sheer abandonment that only free flowing alcohol can produce.

The next to leave unexpectedly was Barry. He had worked for Terry on and off for the last six years and, being a northerner, they got on extremely well. Terry's accent always seemed to broaden dramatically when Barry was around. Terry went outside to see why he was departing prematurely and Barry explained that he had been working for Pierre-Daniel, or PD, the paysagiste (gardener). PD had been nagging Barry all of the previous week to visit a certain bar in La Mouche. This bar was well known for its eclectic clientele and had a reputation for being a gay bar. So, Barry had politely declined PD's offer of a swift half after work each day and was thinking of looking for employment elsewhere.

He was leaving, he hurriedly explained whilst looking over his shoulder, because after consuming copious amounts of wine PD had pinned him in the corner with promises of work whilst trying to stroke him. Barry was not impressed and, being from Burnley, had let PD know in no uncertain terms, by punching him on the nose.

As Barry hurriedly drove off, he cried though the open window of his car, "anyway, who would be the feminine one, he is not even good-looking!"

"Where was PD now?" I enquired.

Terry said that he was with the Dutch lesbians. Good, I thought, at least he can't get into too much trouble there. With astonishment, I looked over and saw Elaina gently wiping his bloodied hooter, as he contentedly fondled her all-encompassing bosom.

11th February

At last Annie came to stay, I couldn't wait to see her it had been too long, we had a lot of catching up to do.

Mind you I'm glad it wasn't a whole week, I don't think my liver could have taken much more. We got so drunk we had to text Sarah to find out who had won X Factor, even though we were watching it.

Annie is looking for love on the Internet and she showed me her profile. I was fascinated; people can wink at you and everything! My husband caught the tail end of the conversation and thought it was a completely different Internet site.

So we trawled through the men that were in her age range. She commented that they all looked so old. I just looked at her; we are old now, aren't we? She said she hadn't thought of that.

There were a few who had winked at her and she had winked back - she even had a few dates lined up.

One potential date who she was chatting to, had said his best feature was his hands. So Harry 'The Hands' was the one, and she arranged to meet up with him the following week.

Her son is in the Marines and off in March to Afghanistan for his first six months, which she is dreading. I'm not sure how you cope with that, but she said she was planning on drinking lots of wine.

15th February

Valentine's Day (for some)

Living with a Yorkshire man you learn to expect nothing so that way you're never disappointed.

I woke up and I was disappointed. Sheepishly, Terry said that he didn't think they sold Valentine's cards in France.

Mind you, he did have a nice little surprise Valentine's treat for me; he had promised Colin, the Jehovah's Witness, that we would attend one of their meetings that night at Kingdom Hall. Terry is always keen to explore new ideas, hence the reason we are on the Scientology mailing list.

On one occasion, he had ended up in the Bournemouth Scientology mission where they did some tests on him and concluded that if he purchased L Ron. Hubbard's book he would be in for some self-salvation. I thought he had just wasted ten quid and that we could have bought a Marks and Spencer's curry with it, but that's Terry for you - he likes all things spiritual.

Nevertheless of we went to the meeting at Kingdom Hall and after two hours bible study I had really had enough. I'm not a great fan of religion - don't get me wrong, I think Jesus was a cool guy, I mean he was a carpenter hippie, didn't care about possession's and was kind to prostitutes. In many ways he reminded me so much of my husband.

I only found out a couple of years ago that the first date he ever took me on was because he was afraid of losing his job.

After moving to Devon, I had made friends with the owners of the caravan park as we were in the same business. They had felt sorry for me and taken me under their wing. I had kicked my husband out and was on my own with children of four and eight years old, twelve thirty-five year old flats and a bar that had seen better days.

I think they thought I would be back off to London before the first of the summer tourists had arrived, (I was tempted).

But with help from my Mum and Dad, I somehow got through those first weeks; mind you it wasn't without excitement. A nice young man and his dog had rented one of the flats paying upfront for six weeks rent on my first day as the new owner.

He was into night fishing and would sit and have coffee in my kitchen whilst palming me off with some undesirable sea creature he hoped I would enjoy. However, when he had failed to turn up for a Court appearance the police arrived on my doorstep looking for him. He had done a runner.

I was an emotional wreck at that time as I had just found out about my husband's affair. Mum and Dad were staying with me as I tried to come to terms with what was happening to the children and me.

The copper leading the investigation, had chatted me up and invited me out for a drink, so Mum and Dad offered to clean out this guy's flat while I went on a date with Mr. Plod, hoping it would cheer me up.

When we got back mum told us,

"It's all done we've had to throw everything away, including the dog's bed as it stunk."

She then went on to say that hidden in the wardrobe were loads of strange blocks of something that seemed to resemble tar. So, with police presence already there and wanting to make a good impression, we went to investigate.

Mr Plod informed us it was cannabis and we quickly realized what all that night fishing was about.

When I told Terry he said it would probably have been worth about thirty thousand pounds. At that time I was in so much financial difficulty, it would have been the answer to my prayers.

In fact the copper didn't amount to much, he was married and came on to lonely women - apparently he was notorious for it. So not only did I lose my potential windfall, I also had my faith in men severely dented once again. I vowed that I would remain single.

My friends at the caravan park had different ideas and, knowing that I would be alone for yet another weekend, they set me up with a date.

Terry asked me to go to a local music festival with him that Saturday night, (my crying had not put him off then). Despite my apprehension I was so excited. It was a warm summer's evening and as the sun went down and the full moon came up we talked, laughed, danced and drank.

We actually got on unbelievably well and, to my surprise, I had the most romantic night of my life - everything was perfect. Terry drove me home and, not wanting to spoil the start of something special, I kissed him on the cheek and thanked him for a magical night and sent him on his way. I was dancing on air and had to telephone Annie to tell her all about it.

It was two years ago that I found out he had been paid to take me out by his boss. Perhaps I should threaten to leave him, and then he might take me to a posh restaurant and not to Kingdom Hall.

On second thoughts, after ten years of marriage he might call my bluff and call it a day. - I couldn't face another divorce, even if it is a great diet, they should market it 'the divorce diet'.

16th February

Took Sam for a walk in the spring sunshine. The daffodils have started to peep up through the cold earth and it always cheers me up to see that the first signs of spring are on their way and that soon the warm sunshine will return. Sadly my idyllic walk was cut short, as the hunters were out shooting anything that moved, not wanting to be on tonight's menu, we headed home.

Mum phoned. She said that she had been to see Gran and that it had all been very stressful. Apparently Gran had called all her children in separately, explaining that she had some very sad news.

Fearing the worse they all went to hear what she had to say.

"This is very upsetting not only for me but for you too, so I'll come straight to the point," Gran had said looking tearful and very serious, "your dad has another woman."

Wow! What a revelation, as Grandad has been dead for six years. How reassuring - heaven must be fun, lucky old Grandad! My Mum then explained this to her and she said,

"I know he's dead, I'm not stupid. I was there when they cremated him!"

Mum was happy though as my Dad won three hundred pounds on the football pools. A holiday was therefore on the cards and Gran would have to deal with Grandads infidelity on her own.

After leaving home at age eighteen, I would return home on a regular basis to see Mum and Dad and catch up with my shopping - you can't beat Leicester for shopping. I would go home, unpack and immediately be on the next Midland red bus into either Leicester or Hinckley and sometimes Nuneaton.

It was on one of these trips that I first spotted my Grandad; you could hardly miss him, he was sporting a bright purple shell suit, gold medallion, white Nike trainers and an overcoat, with his cap at a jaunty angle on his head. A Co-Op shopping bag gave the finishing touch to his bright ensemble. After we had exchanged our hellos and I had got over the shock of seeing him like this, not to mention the strong aroma of Brut aftershave emanating from him, I asked him what he was up to.

"Since I fell out with that thieving git of a bookmaker in the village I have been forced to go elsewhere, it's playing havoc with my betting regime," he explained.

"It's a good job I've got a free bus pass or I'd be buggered, I have been forced to have to travel now to place a bet, would you believe that? That man that calls himself a bookmaker in the village is nothing more than a swindler, you can't trust him, and he's only in it to make himself money, rob you blind he would." he explained incredulously.

My Grandad was obviously very upset about something. Then his mobile phone rang (I had no idea he had one).

"Oh hello Mrs Wong, yes I can pick up some fresh ginger. I'll stop off at Narborough Road. I'm just on my way back home, want to get away before the school kids get out, bloody little sod's - they won't get up and give you a seat."

I looked suspiciously at him and asked "Mrs Wong, what's all that about?"

"Oh she's teaching me to cook, I'm doing spring rolls today, hence the ginger. Your Gran has gone quite off cooking since I retired, she just wants to stay indoors and watch Jeremy Kyle." He answered.

"Oh I see, well good luck then." I said, shocked and too scared to ask why he was going around town looking like a cross between Jimmy Savile, David Icke and Arthur Askey. I thought he might think I was being rude and prying, so I kept quiet.

Later that day I popped round to see Gran, as mum had said she was a bit down in the dumps. I thought it might cheer her up to see the bargains I had bought in Leicester that day. Grandad came in while I was there and I was relieved to see that he was back in his normal attire of man-made fiber slacks, an old Ben Sherman shirt and a jumper that looked like my Gran had knitted it before the war. The only item of clothing that had not changed was his cap.

The following day he was at it again, this time it was in Hinckley,

"Oh hello Grandad, out betting?" I inquired.

"That's right me duck, got a dead cert accumulator for the three-thirty at Kempton," he replied excitedly.

He was dressed in the same alarming way as the day before, only on this occasion his shell suit was a bright turquoise. I couldn't help noticing he was also carrying his library books comprising, Ken Hom's Chinese Cookery Made Easy, The Beginner's Guide to Speaking Mandarin and the latest Len Deighton.

As we stood chatting (I was getting used to his new image by now), his phone rang.

"Oh hello Mrs. Wong, frozen peas yes, no problem, they're on offer - buy one get one free in Iceland. Yes, I'll pop over when I've put me bet on and see you about two thirty." He told her.

"More cooking lessons?" I inquired, this time showing more suspicion.

"Egg fried rice today, me duck," he said.

"Your Gran won't come out - she's addicted to that Jeremy Kyle. She said it's a good one today - ten ways to spot if your other half is cheating," he said innocently.

"Anyway as she's gone off it, cooking I mean, I thought I would treat her for our anniversary and learn to cook her favourite meal as a surprise. That's why Mrs. Wong is helping me, so keep it to yourself," he said, tapping his nose.

"It's spring rolls to start, chicken and cashew nuts with egg fried rice. Then I'm pushing the boat out with crispy duck and pancakes, you can get them off the market, you don't have to fuss about making them, but you mustn't forget the hoi sin sauce" He explained to me.

"It's so easy; you just put the duck in the oven for four to five hours and voila!" He carried on, "Then a nice chocolate cake from the Co-op, as she's not keen on Lychees"

It sounded good, I was most impressed and I bet Gran would be. I can only ever remember eating vegetables that had been boiled to death and covered in salt, or everything else they ate seemed to have been cooked in lard. This would make a welcome change I'm sure.

He must have had a secret changing room like Mr. Ben, as he was always back in his normal clothes when I saw him at home later.

I had no idea if my Gran knew about his fetish for dressing like Ali-G. I never did find out and after he died there was no trace of his garish dressing-up outfits.

I had a theory that as he had been banned from the village betting shop, he went to visit alternative out of town bookies and disguised himself in the hope that no one would recognize him. He could not risk being barred from any other bookies. We didn't have the Internet in those days, so a personal visit was needed to place your bet. The other alternative was to place your bet over the phone and I don't think that was an option for him, as Gran would have soon realized that he was gambling his pension away. You could also get a nice cup of tea in most of the bookies and watch the racing in the warm. It is so easy now; a compulsive gambler need not leave his living room, or have to go out wearing fancy dress.

20th February

Took Ashley and Sophie to the airport and they were so excited. Off to England to Ashley's step mum's birthday party. Sophie still didn't have a coat and it was freezing. What is it with the younger generation and their lack of warm clothing? They must have a different thermostat to us. I commented that it was snowing in England and that they weren't going to the Caribbean. She just shrugged and got on the plane to her idea of freedom (Primark and takeaways). I suppose she must keep warm on mashed potatoes.

Sam was pleased to see us when we got home, but had managed to eat another pair of my slippers whilst we had gone. As usual, his bone lay untouched - these pet shops have a lot to answer for.

24th February

Terry wanted to go and see my brother in Brittany and take his Christmas goodies to him, but I was just not in the mood.

"Come on it'll do you good to get out the house," he reassured me.

I wasn't sure if I was in the mood to be bombarded with his mad conspiracy theories. Since his wife left him with three children to look after five years ago he has steadily become more and more obsessed. I was so glad when Barack Obama was elected, it finally shut him up about George Bush. It's quite wearing and last Christmas they came to stay along with my Mum and Dad and I nearly killed him. I explained that Christmas day was not the time to have a stand up row about the American political system.

Sid, my brother, says he gets overexcited, as living in Brittany most of his friends are French and therefore it's difficult to have deep and meaningful conversations with them, unless it's about wine or how superb the French cheese is, so naturally when he does see us he's on full pelt and on a mission to save our souls from the corrupt politicians and the society which surrounds them.

The last time I saw him he gave me a book:

The post-petroleum survival guide (and cookbook) Recipes for Changing Times because, he kindly explained, "When it all kicks off, Kaz, the supermarkets won't be open."

He was perfectly serious with this warning. He also insisted that I stock up on canned food with a long shelf life and told me that he had warned my Mum to do the same.

However, the last time I went to visit him we did have a catastrophe as our dog, Sam, ate one of his kittens. That didn't go down too well with the children, but my brother said I had done him a favour as he was overrun with them.

27th February

Woke up this morning and discovered that the mice who live in the cupboard next to the fridge have made a bungalow out of the mouse poison container, the two glass bowls the old poison was in, some concrete and a couple of bits of wood that looked just like beams for the roof.

I was most impressed we have very clever mice.

Sarah phoned, she and her boyfriend have bought a pet. It's a Bearded Dragon so I had to have a look online to see what it was like. Not my cup of tea, but then I'm more of a furry sort of pet owner. It eats live locusts and veg, but apparently theirs is not keen on veg (a bit like my Dad) - told her to watch Super Nanny for some tips.

We are off to Istanbul soon, a treat for her 21st birthday. It may be a punishment for me though, as that girl can shop for England.

She has booked the tickets and we will be flying with British Airways from Terminal 5 at Heathrow, God help us. No doubt we'll get caught in a strike and, if we do get there, we won't have any luggage. Gordon Ramsey has a restaurant there, so we've booked in for lunch before our flight. I'm looking forward to asking, "where's my fucking food?"

28th February

Alana and her boyfriend, Les called in this morning. They own one of the holiday cottages at the end of our lane. She was looking a little flushed (not unusual) and I could smell the alcohol on her breath from where I was sitting. I asked her if she would like a coffee, but she declined and informed me that she had brought her own tea bag with her and would only need some boiled water.

She had just called in for a chat and to catch up, it was their first visit since the winter and they had come over to check the house out and feed the mice.

I apologized for the cold kitchen we were sitting in, explaining that we could only afford to have the central heating on for a few hours in the evening.

"Oh don't worry about that it's practically tropical in here," Alana exclaimed.

Les told me that over Christmas the fridge in their house in England had stopped working, so he called into Currys and a helpful assistant (his first day) explained that the room has to be a certain temperature otherwise it wouldn't work. Les said that as their kitchen was practically a greenhouse with all the glass in it, they were lucky if it would reach nine degrees during winter.

He had therefore gone home and moved the fridge into the lounge next to the open fire and, sure enough, it started working again. Well Alana didn't like it; she said that it was far too modern in the room.

However, after she put a nice chintz table cloth over it, along with the Christmas tree she almost forgot it was a fridge and commented that it was really handy for the wine.

Alana is a "Brocanteur" she sells antiques or, as Terry puts it, a load of old rubbish. He says I'm the only person he knows who can go for a nice walk in the countryside and come back having bought a piano

I quite like her rubbish, she has a good eye for shabby chic, I can call in for a cup of boiled water (no coffee allowed on the premises) and come back having spent a small fortune on some smelly worm-eaten pieces of furniture or rusted old iron work.

Alana has a shop near Stonehenge and comes over to France to source her wares. In her unique exotic style, she swishes about in her long flowing paisley patterned skirts, (which have usually seen better days, much like the stuff she sells), and her hair tied up with silk scarves and bright taffeta ribbons, beads and bangles jangling away, making more noise than a Morris dancer. She is a cross between an exotic belly dancer, and Madame Zi Zi who has a booth on Brighton pier.

Les is on the short side, with Jesus sandals on his grubby feet and a beer belly which is usually encased in an over tight slogan emblazed T-shirt.

Today's read 'Don't worry it only seems kinky the first time'. He was however normally sober (well, someone had to drive) while she was inevitably out-of-it or hung over. With her long, flowing home-dyed auburn hair with bits of it missing like a mangy old tom cat, her herbal cigarettes never far from her badly applied lipsticked mouth, she was a sight. They both looked like a couple of old washed-up hippies. I loved to see them, and they made my day.

She also has a 'plummy' English way of speaking - very Public Schoolgirl, all cut glass vowels enunciating her conversations with 'rather', 'I say', 'darling' and 'super'.

My children love Alana's visits too, enjoying chatting to her and winding her up, mainly, especially Sarah who, being a public schoolgirl herself reverts to 'what, what, what, oh, gosh I don't believe it!'

We also use her as a warning to the children of how you can end up if you take drugs. She certainly must have expanded her mind in the sixties and seventies - no one could be that out-of-it without substantial chemical misuse.

Nowadays though I think alcohol is the drug of choice, being so much more socially acceptable and easier to access.

Anyway she told me she had some nice baskets for sale in her giant old Volvo. So, after searching through the bizarre contents of her car we found them and I bought one. Well, someone has to supplement her habit.

28th February

Ashley and Sophie came back worn out (still no coat). They had made it into London to see the sights, even visited Tin Pan Alley, home of all the music shops. They were in rapture, they had been out for all the foreign cuisine England has to offer and which we ex-pats miss so much.

"How was the party?" I asked.

"Brilliant, yeah, really great." Ashley said. Sophie nodded in agreement.

"We stayed at a really posh hotel for the party and had our own room. We ordered up room service, Sophie had some mashed potatoes."

I knew she'd miss that coat.

That night sitting huddled up next to the wood burner, with a cheeky little number from the Noz, I looked back over the month's diary entries. As I slurped my wine I realized I had been living more in the past these last weeks than the present, I could sense the hopelessness that appeared to be taking over.

It was startlingly apparent. My self-enforced isolation was wrapping itself around me like an all-consuming fog. I had to break free of this.

At least next month I had my trip away with Sarah, to look forward to. Hopefully that would break the monotony. Ashley was back now too so that would give me something to do and perhaps, I thought as the wine started to warm me, maybe, I could persuade Terry to consider thinking about moving?

Infidelity, Anniversaries and Istanbul

March 1st

The mice must have had a fight - they have now built a pair of semi-detached bungalows in the dog food cupboard. No wonder I thought I was getting through vast amounts of animal feed, I have been unwittingly supplying the local rodent population.

Haven't broached the subject of moving with Terry yet, he keeps going on about how much of my maintenance money I've squandered, paying for me and Sarah to go to Turkey. I said, I thought that's why the children's father paid it so that I could treat the kids.

"What's wrong with the Zoo?" he asked.

I think if I mentioned a move he would have a seizure. It will have to wait until after the holiday, otherwise he will start moaning, or worse we'll end up having an almighty row and that will be it. I will spend the rest of the time while I'm away brooding.

Sometimes it's best to keep your thoughts to yourself. There would be plenty of time to talk about "our plans" when I came back and who knows he might have missed me. With all the duty free fags, I would surely be flavour of the month. This would be to my advantage, he would be putty in my hands. Yeah right…

Walked the dog and bumped into Alana and Les. They had just finished packing up their overloaded Volvo and explained that they had no time to stop, as they were running late for the ferry.

They had popped over for the weekend to go to a brocante in the Loire.

"Nous avons une week-end splendide, very très bien!" she gushed, attempting to show off her Franglais and enveloping me with her parfum de garlic and stale wine.

I enquired if they had brought paraphernalia over from England to sell at the fair.

"Oui, bien sur – les Français adore les objets Anglais. In fact, darling, I swear you could sell them anything with a Union Jack on it!" she laughed, enjoying her own witticism, as she managed to trap half of her moth eaten sarong in the rusty car door.

I found it difficult to imagine snobby Alana selling anything so gauche. Popping his head out of the boot of the car, a sweaty Les piped up in his guttural gravelly tones.

"Yeah, we flog the 'Frogs' some right old English tat!"

Alana was clearly annoyed by his indiscretion and immediately retorted, winding the passenger window down and bellowing,

"I think you will find, Les, that what I sell are objet d'art. N'est pas?"

I asked if she had any chests of drawers for sale, she said she would keep an eye out for me and see what she could find (that would cheer Terry up, more crappy, worm-eaten furniture).

I watched them depart, weaving down the road in their elderly Volvo which was groaning under the weight and looking like a junk shop on wheels. I could hardly imagine what the Douanes would make of them when they arrived at the port. Do you need a license to import scrap metal to England? I pondered as I walked home.

My Mum and Dad will be celebrating their 50th wedding anniversary on the eighteenth and Sarah emailed me to say that she had googled it and apparently it is a golden anniversary.

I said we would send them a bouquet of flowers and that she was to ask for a gold and cream theme, but definitely no lilies, as Dad hates the smell. Sarah said she would order them, as it is a lot cheaper than sending them from France. I told her to remember to tell them that her Gran was a florist, so we wouldn't put up with a sloppy job.

I am very excited about Istanbul. I asked if she had heard the news about British Airways going on strike. She said she had not seen the news for a couple of weeks. Good job, I thought, as Turkey had experienced an earthquake last week. I was beginning to wonder if this trip was doomed.

March 12th

Just heard the news on the radio that British Airways cabin staff are going on strike on the 20th of March, which is the day we fly, and are striking again on the 27th when we fly back, great!

Phoned Sarah, but she said not to worry as she had heard they'd put extra staff on - she is so gullible. I didn't really want the plane flown by someone drafted in fresh from a crash course in flying.

Apparently the lizard still won't eat his veg.

"Now you know what it's like being a mum," I told her.

Mum and Dad's flowers have been ordered and she told me that she had insisted there were to be no lilies and had remembered to mention that my Mum was a retired florist.

"I just hope Interflora isn't planning industrial action," I told her.

Mum phoned, her first words being "BA are on strike when you fly."

She'd been to see my Gran, who jealously informed her, "That other woman of his must have a car! He goes out every day and she comes and picks him up, but I've not a bloody clue where they get to all day! The trouble with your Dad, our Marlene, is that he just won't accept he's dead!"

Mum sighed, she had stopped trying to correct Gran and argue with her, it was too much like hard work. She said she came away after visiting her not knowing what was real and what wasn't.

"It's like I'm the one with Alzheimer's," she explained, "sometimes I feel like your Grans right and she has got it all sorted out then the fresh air hits me and I have to pull myself together and get a grip on reality. Visiting your Gran these days is like being in a very bad Woody Allen film."

Despite these unnerving revelations Gran was in a good mood. She told Mum the Queen had been to visit her yesterday and that they'd had a lovely chat. Elizabeth, as my Gran fondly called her, was wearing a beautiful powder blue two-piece and tea and cakes had been served to them by Kas the Polish care worker. She said that the only down side was that my Grandad had missed it on account of his carrying on with that other woman.

"Fancy missing tea with the Queen for a bit of how's-your-father with that floozy!" my Gran had cried, annoyed and she vowed to give him a good telling-off the next time he showed up.

I miss my Gran and our chats.

When we moved to our new house from the flat, we were on the same street as my Grandma and Grandad. In fact, most of my family was within spitting distance if I think about it – aunts, uncles and cousins everywhere.

Gran and Grandad had four children, my Mum who was followed by three boys - my beloved uncles. They loved to wind me up and tease me; they introduced me to Rod Stewart, climbing trees, bird nesting, keeping budgies and the thrills of owning an air rifle.

I loved them to bits and would try to hang out and follow them, but I was usually sent home. Especially when they were out on some of their more dangerous missions like riding motor bikes in the back field, swimming in the old disused quarries or getting the boy across the road to try to ride a cow.

My poor Gran and Grandad - those boys nearly killed them. If it wasn't one of them up to no good, it was the other. They were always into some kind of mischief and Grandad was forever bailing them out and keeping the peace.

I now also had my baby brother to look after and, after leaving behind my domestic and gardening duties at the flat, I took on another role as my brother's main carer. I talked for him for the first few years of his life, carried him around before he could walk (and after) washed him, dressed him (usually in my doll's clothes - he and the cat had to share) and played with him. I adored him. He was my real life baby doll, but there was only one problem - he was a boy and I really would have preferred a baby sister.

So he would often be seen in a nice pink dress and lacy tights, to which my mum would screech in horror and rescue him. I would then run to my Gran's house and she would give me biscuits to comfort me and an ear into which I could vent my frustrations about my mum.

I would love to be able to spend more time with her now, listening to her tales of when she was a young girl and working as an usherette in the privately owned village cinema.

Part of her job involved riding her bicycle to the cinema owner's house during the interval to put their chickens to bed. She hated this because she was terrified of the dark and it involved her having to go down their enormous garden with only a flashlight. She had to be really speedy, as she had to be back to show people to their seats before the second half started.

Another time she had told me how she got the scar on her nose by crashing her bike into a Midland red bus. Her favourite tale, however was about how she nearly married the wealthy owner of the local hardware store. She always sighed at this point and told me that we would have been so rich if only she had married young Bertie Bloom. Oh I miss those tales.

March 15th

Things to do:

Post bills

Take library books back

Post Mum and Dad's anniversary card (Golden!)

Clean EVERYWHERE (again)

Took Sam for a walk. It really was the most glorious spring afternoon, the hedgerows are full of yellow primroses and wild daffodils fill the banking around the fields.

It looks just like how I imagine Wordsworth's wife saw it when she described it to her husband and he wrote the poem. The sun was quite warm on my back and, after a brisk run through the fields (trying to lose a bit of weight for my holiday and Sam has over indulged during the winter too), we were both panting and out of breath.

My English neighbour, who has a holiday home at the end of our lane, spotted us and invited us in for tea, I was most grateful and even Sam, got a bowl of water and a biscuit. She is over for the weekend and I am getting a lift with her when she returns to England. The final arrangements were made for the journey, we would be leaving at midday Monday now, that gave us plenty of time to get to the ferry-port as she told me she hated rushing.

Excitedly I ran home and phoned Annie. During the conversation I mentioned the move to her.

"What does Terry think? I thought he was happy with his Cinema and his Harley," she asked.

"I haven't told him yet."

"What do you mean TOLD him? You mean you haven't discussed it yet?"

"I just need to find the right time, you know convince him and everything, make it seem like it's his idea."

"Well good luck with that one, I think you might find he has other ideas, didn't he want to move to Spain?"

"Greece, he wants to eventually retire to Greece, but that's a long time off. There's no way we can be pensioned off yet and I couldn't bloody work in that heat, it would kill me, as for Sam, we'd have to shave him. You don't see many hairy dogs in hot countries, do you?"

She asked if I would be able to visit, as her son is returning to his barracks this weekend; ready for deployment to Afghanistan on the twenty-first.

"Good job they're not flying with British Airways," I told her.

I said I could come early and stay over if she wanted me too as we are leaving on Monday now. I am so relieved I had cleared the winter growth from my legs - must have known I'd be going earlier than planned. At this time of the year it usually takes about three attempts to get rid of my seasonal stubble.

Oh the joys of living in jeans and wellies. You don't get much opportunity to be glamorous here and if you do it's too bloody cold to wear anything revealing, even winceyette pyjamas are obligatoire in a French country bedroom. I can't imagine Normandy housewives wearing peek a boo bras, negligées or naughty knickers, well not the housewives I know.

I asked Annie how Harry the Hands was. She said she had been on a couple of dates, but was put off by the plaque on his teeth, I imagine it reading, 'here died dental hygiene 1995'.

She said she isn't really into dating at the minute and with her son, Paul, off to Afghanistan, she can't imagine having a relationship.

She must be really worried, perhaps I should get two boxes of wine in.

Spoke to Sarah and told her about Annie's sex life (or lack of it) and she told me to shut up.

"Too much information mum," she said through gritted teeth.

I told my mum, "I thought I would be able to talk to Sarah about sex, you know, the younger generation and all that."

"Oh the young, they think they invented sex," Mum laughed.

"Really," I replied, "round here they think the French did. At least Bruno does!"

"You sound much more cheerful" my mum carried on.

I couldn't tell her about my big plan to try and get us to move, she's worse than me for keeping secrets and that's saying something.

"Yeah, I've been keeping a diary; you know writing about my feelings, not bottling things up. It seems to be working, I sort of feel a lot brighter" I added.

"Writing? I don't know where you get that from. Anyway I didn't think you were any good at that sort of thing? As for feelings," she carried on, "we never had them our generation, we just got on with it! Oh, our Karen, have you thought anymore about taking up knitting?" she stressed. "Did wonders for your auntie Jayne; She was a bit like you all "yearnings and emotions" before she had it all taken away. Kept her mind occupied and she made me a lovely twin set."

"Thanks mum," I sighed.

Mum had been to see Gran, who had developed a liking for Desperate Housewives and Sex in the City. Mum said she'd be saying 'no shit' next, complete with an American accent. Anyway, Mum had been to the local charity shop and managed to pick up series three of Desperate Housewives for only a fiver. She said she would have a look on eBay later for Sex in the City DVDs.

I wondered if Gran would like the film, but Mum said that she would be likely to nod-off half way through. An episode at a time is all she can manage, otherwise she does not know where she is.

Terry will be in charge of Sam while I am away, so I think I'll hide all the bathmats, cushions and slippers otherwise I might be upset on my return and I don't think either of them want that.

March 18th

Phoned Mum and Dad from Annie's to wish them a happy anniversary and Dad mystified me by saying thank you for the flowers and that he had put them in the loft.

I was thoroughly confused until he explained,

"You silly idiot, it's our forty-ninth this year not our fiftieth!"

"So why was Mum going on about what she was going to do then? You know, have a big party or go on holiday. When you booked that holiday I thought, oh that's it, that's what you are going to do to celebrate," I blustered.

"No," Dad said, "you know what your Mum is like. She just has to plan everything well in advance. Anyway, the flowers are lovely and we'll take a photo so you don't have to bother sending any next year."

NOTE: Does this mean that they want a big party next year? Must start saving.

Mum e-mailed me a photo of the flowers. They had put lilies in the bouquet, so I won't be using that florist again.

March 30th

At last back home in Normandy again after my trip with Sarah. I nearly didn't make it to England. It was my own fault - when you agree to take a lift with someone else you really are at their mercy.

68

We had arranged to leave at midday in order to allow plenty of time to catch the ferry. At midday, my neighbour phoned to say she was running late.

She eventually arrived an hour late saying that we still had plenty of time. We then had to get petrol - no problem, still loads of time. What she forgot to mention was that the dilapidated van we were travelling in was on its last legs and therefore it was not advisable to turn off the engine as it may not start again.

She turned off the engine and, sure enough, it failed to start, nothing - it was dead. Not to panic. I looked at my watch - it was fine, we still had two hours to get to Caen. We proceeded to ask anyone we could find if they could help by giving us a jump-start. Not knowing what this is in French, it made a very interesting mime involving jumping up and down, throwing ourselves forward whilst pointing at the van and going vroomm, vroomm.

After a few shrugs, bemused looks and mutters about the bizarre Anglais, an attractive, young French girl came over to see if she could help.

She seemed to understand our predicament and jumped in her car, whilst indicating that she would be back to help us. She quickly returned with a portable jump-starter, borrowed from her friend up the road who was a garagiste. The van spluttered reluctantly into life and, hey presto, we were on our way. She had been so accommodating and generous. The episode had restored my faith in the youth of today.

With a warm feeling in our hearts we flew up the A84 like a bat out of hell. We now only had an hour before sailing. I did not dare to look at my watch and we made it with only seconds to spare. With some reluctance they loaded us on and slammed the bow doors shut.

I could hardly believe we had made it and promptly headed to the bar for a large gin and tonic and several cigarettes. I was very grateful to my neighbour for the lift, but vowed never to accept one again - this was far too stressful.

"They always wait a bit later for the stragglers, I do this all the time and I haven't missed a ferry yet," she said calmly.

I bet you haven't, I muttered into my gin, thinking I would sooner save the excitement for my holiday, as rally driving is not really my thing. I was really looking forward to spending time with my daughter and she would never have forgiven me if we had missed the ferry and therefore our flights and I wouldn't have blamed her.

She had been planning this holiday with more military precision than Annie's son, Paul, would be experiencing in Afghanistan.

We got to Istanbul and after being put in the wrong hotel for the first night we finally made it to the right one. Great - now we could start to relax, but I had forgotten I was with the Queen of scheduling.

Sarah obviously has my mother's genes and had organized the whole trip. She proudly presented me with a detailed, hour-by-hour itinerary of what we would be doing for the next week. My heart sank - so no relaxing by the pool and enjoying the sauna and steam room then?

"Well you could have a sauna on Tuesday night when we get back from visiting Hagia Sophia," Sarah said, cheering me up.

We went everywhere, saw everything there is to see and some things that you really need not bother with.

Istanbul is wonderful and one of the most beautiful cities I have ever visited - I was so glad Sarah had chosen it. She had certainly done her homework and I was very well looked after, it was like having my own personal travel guide in my pocket. She had researched it all and we really did have an incredible time.

Sarah says I attract nutters, but I like to think I am a friendly sort of person, so people feel at ease chatting to me.

We met a nice retired man from Washington D.C. who invited me to visit America, saying that I would be welcome to stay in his condo. He told us he was very happy with the new President and that, under Barack Obama, he was able to use his pension to visit his nephew in Istanbul.

"I sure couldn't have done that when Bush was in charge," he informed us. I made a mental note to tell my brother, how well Barack was doing.

"No shit," I replied, pleased to get in my Mum's favourite American saying. She would be so proud.

We had dinner and were joined by a nice man from Spain who sold parts for Peugeot and was doing business in the city. He showed us photos of his children and had his photo taken with us, while we finished a bottle of wine he had kindly bought and discussed our mutual love of Land Rovers.

Two back-packers from Israel joined our table, buying a bottle of wine for us to share. They told us about their journey and how they had been ripped-off in a club, by a woman befriending them and then feeling obliged to supply her with free drinks all night. An old trick, I told them.

We then went on to discuss where you could find the cheapest food, MacDonald's, they were everywhere. After finding out they were studying marine biology and climate change, we had a debate about global warming. They agreed it's all a con. I thought of my brother again - he would love it here.

I told them my theory on global warming and the smoking ban.

"Just look around you," I stated. "There are outdoor heaters everywhere. All the bars and restaurants are desperate for you to smoke your fags at their sub-tropical, outside tables. You didn't get calor gas pollution like that when you could smoke inside." I sniggered.

The following night, a handsome blonde guy, Kurt, from Germany joined us for a shisha pipe. He showed us his tattoo, it looked a little sore and bloody but you could just make out the artists impression of the Blue Mosque. A unique souvenir I told him.

We were asked out dancing by a couple of waiters, but we didn't go. By that time in the evening I could only just walk. I was aching from all the day's sightseeing and only just had enough energy to shuffle back to our hotel.

Sarah was happy smoking cheap Turkish cigarettes and stroking the numerous cats that were curled up warming themselves under the outside heaters.

As she was tickling their ears and watching them contentedly snuggling up to her, our waiter Mohammed told us, "It was like

71

Beirut here last week, and they were all 'at it'. They were howling like banshees and shagging everything in sight; it was really putting off our customers."

It was like watching a David Attenborough documentary, as he described, complete with actions in case we hadn't understood, what these sex crazed moggies had been up to.

So all in all it had turned out to be quite a cultural trip.

Mind you, the trip to the Cagaloglu Turkish Baths was an experience I will not forget in a hurry. After Fatima, in name and stature, had stripped me of my bikini, explaining that it would spoil my treatment, she made me lay face down on the hot marble and commenced to pummel me with her sponge and fists. I thought I was going to be abused, murdered and dumped in the Bosphorus. I had never felt so violated in my life – this woman had obviously been trained by the Marquis de Sade.

She then joined me in my nakedness by removing her sarong and, with no hint of embarrassment, started to firmly rub her ample bosoms over my body. Soapsuds were flying everywhere and I did not know whether to laugh or cry at what I had got myself into. My gasps of horror were inaudible over the noise of her slapping breasts.

I suddenly thought of Sarah, if this was what was happening to me, how was she coping? In the steam-filled, echoing marble room I could only just make out her silhouette. They had her too! We were surely being thoroughly cleansed ready to be sold to Arab sex-slave traders.

Fatima pushed me face down onto the circular, raised Goebektas Platform, which was in the centre of the room, informing me that she was leaving me to work up a sweat! On her return, she proceeded to jab me, prod me and pull my arms and legs out of their sockets

To my horror, she then straddled my backside and, with her naked form, continued with this barbaric Turkish ritual. I closed my eyes, praying that it would soon be over. No such luck, as Sarah had insisted that we book the 'Deluxe Service'. Involuntary whimpers of pain were now escaping from my tender and bruised body.

Eventually Fatima pulled my head around, forcing me to open my eyes. Unknown to me, we had now been joined by a coach load of Japanese tourists who were now in various stages of torture. The stone platform on which I lay resembled a tableau from an Ingres painting. We were packed head to toe in a circle of nakedness – all with a pretty good view up the next person's thighs. I have never been so grateful to be shortsighted.

Fatima then took me by the hand and led me, like a prize bull, over to the water basins where I received a washing like nothing I had ever experienced. I thought that this must be what it is like when you select the 'super-plus' option at the car wash.

She scrubbed me with her rough, coarse mitt and seemed determined to remove the outer layers of my epidermis. She soaped me up again and roughly washed my hair and even had a good root around inside my ears. I have never been so clean.

I started to feel a little more relaxed and comfortable, happy in the knowledge that, although I was naked, there were only women in the room as men were forbidden. Apparently the penalty was death for any man who dared to enter. I hoped the plumbing was okay today.

As Fatima guided me back to the stone torture table, I realised with a heavy heart that my ordeal was not yet over – there was more to come!

Now that I was clean and refreshed, she informed me, the massage could begin. I could hardly contain myself, I thought I was going to faint with fear.

On pummelling my naked flesh she exerted a pressure I didn't know a woman could possess. She repeatedly kneaded and slapped my already raw skin as I lay in a state of shock and exhaustion. Moaning aloud, I wondered if Fatima had got out of bed the wrong side that morning and was taking her frustrations out on me.

Finally it was over and I sighed with relief. Sarah and I were at last reunited. She was having her wet hair combed out by Fatima's even fatter twin sister, who said she wanted to keep Sarah, as she was so beautiful.

I bet, I thought – I know your game – you will have her working for a handful of lira and she will never see the light of day again. I motioned to Sarah, saying let's get out of here. She, however, seemed a lot more relaxed than me.

Back in our hotel, sipping much needed drinks, I asked Sarah if she was okay.

"Wow it was amazing," she replied, "I loved it, I'd have one every week if I could. Mind you," she mused, "I have never had my boobs washed by a stranger before."

I must really be getting old and Sarah must get out more.

Birthdays, Bodies and Boredom

April 2nd

Matthew's birthday

He would have been twenty-two today; I lit a candle by his photo and took the dog for a walk.

April 6th

Sarah's 21st birthday

Sarah and I had celebrated in Istanbul, so she will be out tonight with her friends and having a good time in Notting Hill. Lucky thing. I will still miss her like mad and wish I was with her - I think I always will.

It hadn't been simple though and I had nearly lost her during my pregnancy.

One Friday night after a busy day playing with Matthew and the little boy I was child-minding, I was looking forward to a long soak in the bath.

I had eventually managed to settle Matthew and got him to sleep. I was looking forward to enjoy some peace; wallowing in a warm bath before putting my feet up and watching some rubbish on the telly.

I had a seven-month old baby and I was pregnant again - seventeen weeks pregnant and exhausted. I wasn't that thrilled about it, as I was struggling enough, so how was I going to cope with another baby?

As I ran the bath I realized with horror that I was bleeding. In a state of shock and unsure what was happening, I tearfully phoned my next door neighbour who came round immediately as my Husband was out down the pub. She had three children of her own and was about to become a grandma, so she knew what was what.

She brought her sixteen-year old daughter, Louise, who would stay with Matthew, he was still thankfully fast asleep, whilst her Mum took me to Ashford Hospital. Louise urged me to stay positive and told me there was no way I would lose my baby.

On arriving at the hospital I was examined and informed that as I was bleeding quite badly, it would be necessary to stay there where they could look after me. They told me it was fifty-fifty, I would either miscarry in the night or hold on to my baby and that there was nothing they could do.

I had never been so afraid. I wanted my Mum, but she was miles away in Leicester. I was terrified and felt so very alone. I tried my hardest to stay positive and prayed I would not lose this baby who suddenly meant everything to me, I couldn't comprehend the thought of not having it.

I had been quite flippant about being pregnant again so quickly, but suddenly the magnitude hit me, this was a little life living inside me and it wasn't doing very well. It needed me and I needed it - I was going to fight and hold on to it with all my heart. That night I fell in love with my unborn child, stroking and reassuring it that I did want it and would do anything to keep it.

The next morning I had not miscarried and was taken for a scan to see what was happening. My placenta had slipped down and I had a condition called placenta previa and this is what had caused the bleeding. They advised me that it usually rights itself just as you go into labour, but I would be monitored more regularly and scanned once a month to determine if the baby was still in the same position. I would be able to have a natural birth, but the surgeon would be on standby just in case we needed help.

I stopped child-minding and tried to take life easier – well, as much as is possible with a toddler to look after. My neighbour's daughter helped me, as she was so good with Matthew.

My due date eventually arrived I was summoned to the hospital to have my labour induced. I had chosen to have my baby on Thursday, 6th April as I wasn't keen on Wednesdays, Fridays or odd numbers.

All went well and, as hoped, everything moved in the right direction and a normal birth brought my beautiful, more precious than she would ever realize, baby girl into the world. Her father insisted on calling her Sarah and I added Louise. As long as I live, I will never forget that cold night in November when I had nearly lost her and how my neighbour's caring daughter sat me down with a cup of tea to calm me down and wiped away my tears, never doubting I would be fine. I wanted my daughter to be like that and gave her the name Louise hoping she would have similar qualities.

At last, after all these years, I have just looked up the meaning of the name Louise and was amazed that I had not instinctively realized, it's 'warrior' or 'fighter'. Sarah (princess) Louise (warrior) - princess warrior - it sounds just like something out of a super hero comic, that's my Sarah and, if you knew her, you would agree.

I phoned her and gave her my love. I told her I missed her so much and just wanted to give her a big hug, but I tried not to be too emotional as I didn't want to upset her. I knew that I should have been there with her, if only just to see her for an hour. This was very wrong, and I knew it, I ached for my family and felt that something had to change.

7th April

Took Sam to the vets for his yearly check-up and injections, praying there would be no cats about.

All went well and I have completed the paper work, which now means he is registered as living in France. At least if he gets lost they won't phone Bruno, in Germany, in the middle of the night.

The only hiccup was when the vet put a thermometer up his bum to take his temperature. Unfortunately he is not that keen on you going anywhere near his bottom, so decided to bite the vet. For obvious reasons, this did not endear him to her and, after muzzling him, she declared that he was a dangerous dog;

Ashley explained to the vet that, in fact, he is very gentle and docile (unless you are a cat) and that he had a bad experience as a puppy when he ate some glass. Bruno had told me this and that it had resulted in him having to have an operation on his rear end. Ever since that time he does not like anyone going near that part of his anatomy. Anyway, as Ashley said,

"Who would be comfortable with a stranger putting things up your bum?"

"I think it's the vet who has a problem, not the dog," I reassured Ashley, "he just behaved as we all would under the circumstances. Anyway, I think I will get Terry to take him next year." I muttered.

April 8th

Just been doing a bit of cleaning and trying to find somewhere to put the lamp I bought in Istanbul. Sarah had emailed me a photo of hers and it really looks good in her flat. She had put it on her windowsill between photos of Rage Against the Machine and Marilyn Monroe. I went to put mine on the piano, but decided my Mum's wedding photos looked better there. I gave them a quick dust with my sleeve and smiled at the little bridesmaids in the photo - so cute.

With the cold remains of my cup of coffee, I sat down at the kitchen table. Sam was looking at me, willing me to take him out for a walk - at least the fresh air will do me good, I thought.

Before I could take him, the phone rang. It was my Mum and she had the most unpleasant news, the police had knocked at the door very early that morning to say that they were looking for my Gran.

Mum calmly explained that Gran was in a care home and aged ninety-two. Still in her pyjamas, Mum made the young police officers a coffee and took them into the lounge, where they began to explain what the surprise call was all about.

A body had been found in a flat in London. The deceased had left a note with the name of her next of kin on it - Mary Wileman - my Gran, and also my Mum's name and address. It transpired that it was my Mum's cousin, Joy.

The police had found her after a neighbour had alerted them; it was discovered that she had been dead for about a month.

My poor Mum could hardly comprehend what was being said. We had not heard from Joy for years, ever since she wrote to my Gran and Grandad after her Mum died and stated she didn't want anything to do with her Mum's funeral arrangements. She had asked if my Gran could sort it all out, as she had been advised by her doctor not to have anything to do with the family, as it was detrimental to her health.

I ask you!

Well that didn't go down very well with my Grandad at the time, who was a very decent man. He was very upset by her request and wrote and told her.

Even so, my Gran and Grandad did what was requested of them and arranged everything for Joy's Mum, the funeral and clearing the house of her possessions. They even kept her sewing machine, sheet music, and rusty rabbit cage, in case Joy changed her mind and wanted them back.

The circumstances of Joy's death were not yet fully known, all they could say was that it looked as though she had starved herself to death and there was no foul play involved.

They told her that the Coroner would be in touch and they would take it from there. The policemen left and my Mum broke down, it was such a shock. We all assumed that Joy, who had been a teacher and musician, was having the time of her life living it up in London and enjoying herself.

At one time there had been talk that she was a lesbian. She'd had a big fight with her Mum one Christmas, she had returned home for the festive season, only to find a cold miserable house with little food or comfort. When the bottom fell out of the ancient oven, whilst the turkey was cooking, this had been the final straw. Joy had hot footed it back to London. Leaving behind her dejected Mother, who by now was in a terrible state. My Gran said there was more to it than that, she thought Joy had told her she was living with a woman, which had resulted in Joy and her mother having a blazing row.

Anyway, lesbian or not, she was dead and someone was going to have to sort it all out. As her next of kin, my Gran was legally responsible. However, as she was in a care home, the responsibility would now fall to my Mum, who has Power of Attorney for Gran.

I put the phone down stunned - I couldn't believe it, the shock was unimaginable. All I could think about was how miserable she must have been, to die alone with no one around and then for her death not to be noticed for a whole month. She had no friends or family nearby - she just slipped away and no one cared. She was part of our family and, unaware of her problems, we had not been able to help her. It was wretched.

I couldn't help but think how strange – only minutes before, I had been dusting her photo and looking at her. The little bridesmaid, who had been sitting on my piano all these years and I didn't even know her.

April 9th

Phoned my Mum, she is still really distressed by Joy's death. She had spoken to the Coroner who had explained things in more detail, but Mum would have to travel up to London to sort everything out. It was decided that my Aunt would go with her, they would travel up to London by train next week and stay in a bed and breakfast near St John's Wood. My Auntie Jayne was taking a flask and sandwiches, bin bags and her rubber gloves, so they would be well prepared.

April 13th

Mum phoned and said she had been to see Gran; it was her ninety third birthday and with her carers singing happy birthday to her and making a fuss, she was in her element. She had been a bit disappointed that Grandad had not bothered to turn up, but she said that considering he was still with 'that woman', she was not at all surprised.

"He's been out with her again; she's got a car you know."

Mum has given up telling her that Grandad is dead and did not have another woman. It shocks my Mum, as my Grandad was a thoughtful and charming man, his only affair was with the bookmakers.

"It's so sad that Gran keeps going on about this and won't accept that Grandad has died," Mum protested, "he would never have done anything to hurt her, let alone have an affair. Why couldn't remember the lovely times they had together, all the wonderful holidays they had shared, like when they went to Venice?"

Now, my Gran loves her Sherry - I am not saying she has a problem, she only has the occasional tipple, but before she went to live in the care home she did like to make sure she had a bottle in the house at all times.

So one day, whilst out shopping, my Gran realised that they had forgotten the sherry and Grandad was sent back inside the Co-Op to acquire a bottle.

Well, at the time the Co-Op was running a competition called 'Cluedo', which was based on the board game. Every time you purchased something you were given a scratch card, which revealed combinations of the game - Colonel Mustard in the sitting room with the lead pipe, you get the idea.

Back at home they got out the scratch cards. Gran did hers first, nothing, no matches. Then remembering the second card, given for the sherry, they scratched away. It turned out they had a match and it was the winning combination!

They asked my Mum to check it and she phoned the winners' phone number for confirmation, as my grandparents were both in their eighties at this time.

Yes, they had indeed won! They had won the first prize of a trip to Venice on the Orient Express staying at the Cipriani! They could hardly believe it, they had secured the trip of a lifetime and all because they had forgotten to buy the bloody sherry!

To this day my Gran always sings the praises of a tipple a day, and makes sure my mum still shops at the Co-Op.

April 16th

Mum phoned. She has just returned from London and everything had gone as well as can be expected. There were still lots of unanswered questions, but she found out more about Joy's life. She had managed to trace an old work colleague.

She wasn't a lesbian, but had been a patient at the Priory Hospital and had a history of mental illness. The flat was a mess with nothing of significance; there had been no food in the cupboards just empty packets, hundreds of Tic-Tac boxes and no money. It was still very confusing - had she starved herself to death because she could not afford to eat or had she been gradually and deliberately committing suicide?

They had started to piece together her life. She had walked out of her teaching job shortly after her Mum had died, saying she was being bullied and then had signed on the social. However, the previous November they had stopped all her benefits and she had been existing on her credit cards and bank accounts, which were all now maxed out.

It was painful for my Mum to understand how she had ended up like this, but Mum and Auntie Jayne were doing a fine job. If Rosemary and Thyme decide to hang up their wellington boots then I'm sure Auntie Jayne and Mum could fill them.

They had really become a pair of pensionable detectives, nothing would pass them by and they had resolved to get to the bottom of things.

I felt so useless stuck here in France, but with Ashley's exams round the corner I didn't have a choice, someone had to keep an eye on him.

At least it had started to warm up and the weather was an improvement to my mood. The first of the Vide Greniers (car boot sales) had started, so rummaging around in other people junk would cheer me up. Although if it is anything like last year's efforts they will have just fetched out their rubbish from the previous unsuccessful attempts, and try to sell them this year to some poor unsuspecting tourist, who really didn't know why they had just paid ten euros for a collection of old champagne corks or a bicycle with one wheel. I swear the French are at the forefront of recycling, as they never seem to throw anything away!

This year's annual Fête and Grenier sale didn't disappoint. The road had been cordoned off and there were stalls lining the main thoroughfare in the once sleepy little commune. Noise and smells assaulted our senses as we ventured out of our car, stepping on to the dewy grass, narrowly avoiding fresh cow pats, reminding us the residents must have only moved out that morning. Sam had a good sniff around, taking in the scents of cow shit and burnt sausages emanating from the obligatoire food stand cremating the saucisse et frites. The throng of people perturbed him slightly, but he was still keen to take Terry for a drag round the stalls.

We made it back to the car worn out, our clothes smelling of the food stands with their deep ingrained hot fat, greasy sausages, and billowing clouds of black smoke, polluting the rural countryside.

Terry had expertly deflected Sam away from the cages and cardboard boxes that held a vast array of chickens, rabbits and ferrets, all for sale, and all of which would have made a tasty snack for our dog.

The food stands were cooking up enough saucisses to feed the whole of Normandy and indeed, there seemed to be enough folk there. I had never seen Mesnil Garnier so busy.

On a good day you are lucky to spot a few cars, a handful of tractors and old Jacques on his way back from the boulangerie, with a baguette wedged in one arm, a damp Gauloise in his teeth, blue overalls wrapped around his large belly, and still wearing his slippers. Somehow managing to navigate his ancient Mobylette whilst smiling and waving.

It was good to see Jacques today making an effort for the fête, replacing his slippers for wellington boots. A handsome black beret was perched on his unruly grey hair, the overalls were still de rigueur, and his faithful Gauloise was protruding from the side of his mouth. He was propping up the bar or perhaps the bar was propping him up, as he certainly looked worse for the wear. He was still beaming with his monstrous moustache twitching up and down, his flushed face as he joined in the chorus of Non Je ne Regrette Rien, which was being blasted out of the overhead tannoy system.

April 20th

Ashley's birthday - he is seventeen today. I can hardly believe he has grown up so quickly. He has been my rock and a real friend, I could not have worked out how to use my computer without him. He is off to university next year, preferring to go back to England- and who could blame him? I'm not sure how I will cope when he's not around, especially with the more technical problems.

It really will be the end of an era and we will never have the same times again. I feared an empty nest syndrome and with things not picking up in Normandy, I wasn't sure how I would cope. Just Terry, me and the dog.

I only really started to appreciate my parents when I was in my forties. I suppose you just expect them to always be there and take the shit you throw at them, and I have thrown a lot. Anyway it is a year of firsts, and after spending a week with Sarah on our own I am doing the same with my Mum.

We are off to the Chelsea Flower Show as Mum wanted to take me while she can still walk round and enjoy it without being worn-out out, best not take Sarah then. We will stay in London for a few days and see Sarah and her boyfriend, and Slash the bearded dragon. It will mean that Mum can visit her flat - I do hope she has a tidy up.

April 22nd

My brother's birthday and I phoned to wish him a good one. The kids were on school holidays, so they were going to bake him a cake. We had a discussion about what the government was up to, all bad, of course.

Told him to have a look on Facebook and then he would be able to see our photos from Istanbul. He immediately responded by asking if I knew Facebook was set up by the CIA to spy on us all, and I should warn Sarah not to use it.

He had just dug over his allotment ready to plant it all up.

"You want to get your spuds in Kaz," he informed me, "there's a full moon and it's the optimum time for planting."

Did he mean so that you can see in the dark? I didn't like to ask.

"You sound a bit fed up" I said, detecting a note of gloom in his voice.

"Yeah, Fredrick has moved into the caravan, his wife chucked him out again."

"I thought you got on well with Freddy, is he on a downer?"

"No it's not that, he says he's glad to be free of her, no, he wants to get fit, pump up his muscles. Ludo told him he's so good-looking he could find work as a model."

"Yeah, he is rather gorgeous in a gay George Michael way." I responded.

"So I said to him, instead of lifting weights in my caravan come and help me dig the veg patch, but he won't lift a bloody finger to be helpful, I tell you Kaz, it's like having a bloody camp Popeye living here."

So Fast Freddy was driving my brother mad with his exercise routine and he went on to explain, "Bloody Ludo's no better encouraging him, it will be just like when he applied to be an air steward all over again, I'm telling you Kaz, it'll only end in tears."

April 23rd

Just packed Terry off to work for the day and the house is silent again now. No noise, nothing, the dog has been out and immediately come back in and retired to his bed. What shall I do today to break up the boredom?

I told my neighbour that I hated it here and wanted to move. She said I was mad, that we have a beautiful house and after spending all that time and money renovating it, I should be really happy.

I am happy - just lonely and bored. There is only so much cleaning, baking, shopping and dog walking you can do. I said that it is OK living in the beautiful countryside, but if you can't share it then you could be anywhere trapped and lonely.

She just didn't get it. You have to live here week after week - same old, same old - nothing changes. She was fortunate enough to own a holiday home here, so her situation was very different from mine.

I tried to explain to her that there are two types of ex-pats – runners and losers, all with very good reasons to re-invent themselves, nobody is really as they seem. I knew that I was a runner. I had willingly made every effort to escape my grief-stricken past and my ex-husband in England. I think I hoped that putting the English Channel between us would stop him trying to boss me around. I had no delusions as to why I had made the move, I wanted to put the past behind me.

The problem was, I just did not fit in. I did not fit in with the large group of ex-pats who congregated outside the Bar des Sports and ordered café au lait in loud, English accents. Nor did I fit in with the local farmers' wives who were happy looking after their cows, making Calvados and having heated discussions about whether Sarkozy would go back to his wife now that his mistress had brought out a CD.

I had lost my sense of community and did not seem to be having the wonderful lifestyle I thought I would. I was a fake, pretending to those closest to me that everything was okay. I know I needed to assimilate to fit in, but the only assimilations I was interested in were those in Star Trek.

I was in need of some retail therapy, preferably courtesy of Marks and Spencer's. All the ex-pats miss some shop or other, it's all we ever talk about, that and the state of our fosse-septiques. God knows why, but we are all so obsessed with the state of our toilet disposal systems. Living in the countryside no one has main sewers, so we all have various aged contraptions buried somewhere in our gardens. In-depth discussions about them seem to delight the ex-pats no end.

You can meet someone for the first time and have a nice chat about the weather, shopping in England, where you can get a curry from, and then, sure as anything, the subject will turn to fosse-septiques, their age, how full they are, when to empty them and even how to find it or, indeed, if they even have one. This can go on for hours and sometimes you meet the same people again and the conversation will start right where you left it, back talking about shit again.

No wonder the French think we are mad. At this time of the year they spend many a happy hour spreading the contents of their fosse over their fields, while we are forced to barricade ourselves indoors and close all the windows because of the all-permeating stink.

Just got excited, heard a car on the driveway so went downstairs to investigate, only to find that it was Bruno who had come to check on his cows.

Had an email from a friend a few months ago, I had not deleted it but I hadn't responded either. I had lost touch with her.

When I was at secondary school we were inseparable, she was my best friend. Then when we were fourteen and at that difficult age, her family moved away. I found this really hard as her friendship had been my life, and her leaving had left a great hole. Everyone else had formed tight friendships by then, and as I had put most of my energy into ours, I was left without anyone. We would visit each other in the holidays and we wrote letters, but she had moved on. She was at a good school and doing very well, while I was still struggling with my literacy and often ended up with the kids with learning difficulties, as I just could not spell KAT for the life of me.

She said in her email she was doing well, teaching maths in Birmingham and had three wonderful children, who you could tell were her pride and joy. She sounded happy and content. I was pleased for her, so why was I so reluctant to get in touch? She asked if I went back to Leicester much and what I was up to. I guess that was it - what do you say? 'Oh, you know, just living the dream in Normandy'.

Is this what it is all about? Surfing the net, checking out Facebook, the for sale ads on the ex-pat forum. This is where you find the ads proclaiming 'everything must go' after life has got too much and they simply have to go back to England.

I feel I am spiraling out of control and the dream is turning into a nightmare of loneliness and isolation, I have to do something to change it. A friend recently told me he had built a row of six terraced houses last winter to keep himself sane. I was most impressed, as I didn't have him cut out as a builder. Then he explained, 'In cardboard for my train set'. What a let down.

Writing is my only escape from the real world. It isn't hard work, well not like my building projects and cleaning. I can lose myself for a bit and get lost in my thoughts and it does seem to help. It is difficult to explain how lonely this life is, the solitude just eats you up and when I try to explain to people that I haven't had a conversation with anyone; apart from Terry, the dog, Ashley and waving at the postman, for two months they don't believe me. But it is true, we hardly see anyone. I know a lot of it is my fault, I have become too disheartened to make friends and join the local clique of women. I sort of understand how Howard Hughes got into such a state and Joy for that matter, it is quite easy to opt out.

If you don't make an effort then nobody else will.

Thank goodness I have my writing, but I do not know what I will do when I have written everything down. Perhaps I will have to invent a new life for myself, a sort of alter ego and live out my fantasy existence making it all up. There are certainly enough Brits over here that have done just that. I have never met so many millionaires, old rock stars, actors or professional people as here in Normandy. You only have to walk down the street and you can bump into:

Princess Diana's former body guard

A singer who was in a seventies pop group

A high ranking Commodore (the military type, not Lionel Richie although that would not surprise me)

Countless Actors and Actresses (one who has now retrained and become a chimney sweep - handy if the local ex-pats ever put on a production of Mary Poppins)

A woman who was big in politics in the seventies

Oh and loads of writers - everyone is writing a book, or should I say their memoirs?

Someone, who knows someone who went to school with Hugh Grant (I met her at the hairdressers)

Three millionaires, one of whom has an OBE

I said to a couple I met recently that I felt you really could tell people anything - nobody would ever know you hadn't been a ballerina or a show jumper or played Rugby for Leicester. It was possible to completely re-invent yourself here. It is as if they think, 'So what, I was a failure in the UK, but now I have all this money from selling my house in England, live in a big (if unfinished and falling down) house in Normandy and no one needs to know I was really a shop fitter from Ramsgate'. All of a sudden you are 'Susan, owner of her own designer boutique (frequented by royalty) who once appeared on Come dine with me.'

It's a bit like Stars in Your Eyes (without the singing) – 'Tonight Matthew, I am going to be rich and successful'.

Or there's always the infamous P&O course, which we've witnessed many ex-pats resort to; this consists of a six-hour intense program for anyone leaving the UK to start a new life in Normandy.

9 am - board the ferry in England with no qualifications or experience

10 am - bump into a man in the bar and have a two hour intensive chat with someone who has done the course before and is now happily residing in Normandy - trading as a fully registered and qualified: plumber, carpenter, roofer, painter and decorator, gardener or motor mechanic, hairdresser or beautician (you can take your pick)

As the ferry docks at the port in France – you disembark as a fully qualified artisan. Re-invented and suddenly fully qualified with years of experience, welcome to the P&O ex- pats' bullshit baffles brains trade department. All you'll need is like minded Brits who don't ask too many questions and who are not bothered about seeing your qualifications. As long as they can get their barn renovated at a knock down price they aren't bothered, you have made it and are now a fully paid up member of the re-invention society. A life of ripping off your fellow Brits awaits you.

24th April

Just got back from shopping and I had a proper conversation with a French person who wanted to chat with me. It was the girl on the check-out, she always has a lovely welcoming smile and has always been so friendly to me. Well, just recently we have been bumping into each other in the Noz shop. She asked me if I had been in this week, as they had a lovely stock of china - especially plates and cups. I said I would probably go in on Monday and she said that as that was her day off, she would be calling in as well to add to her china collection and would look forward to seeing me there.

After years of just saying 'bonjour, ça va' and commenting on the weather 'quel temps de cochon!' Or making a joke about not being able to find the right coins quickly enough when paying, 'c'est trop petite pour moi, je détesté les monies', I at last had someone talking to me, I would no longer have to face the indignity of these banal conversations. I love that shop! I vowed to give them more of my custom.

26th April

When we first moved here, Terry went back to Scotland to see his Mum as it was her seventieth birthday. A party had been arranged and all his family would be there.

Ashley and I could not go as he had only just started school here and I did not think they would take kindly to us messing them about. They had gone out of their way to accommodate him in their school after all, especially as he was the only English child there at the time.

Anyway we were on our own for two weeks. Our neighbour had offered to take me shopping and Ashley was picked up by the school bus.

I kept myself busy sorting out our new home, unpacking and exploring the barns and outbuildings. The guy from whom we had bought the house had left countless bits and pieces - there were the whole contents of a woman's makeup bag and toiletries in the attic bathroom, so I busied myself clearing these out.

At night, though, I was plagued with strange feelings and nightmares. They started as dreams and got worse and worse, so that in the end I had Ashley sleeping in bed with me. I was petrified.

It was the same dream every night - a woman would appear and tell me to jump. 'Jump off a cliff, then it will all be over, you will not have to worry anymore,' the voice in the dream would repeat over and over again.

I could take it no longer and when Terry phoned to say that the party had been a success, I begged him to return as soon as possible. I was in tears and pleading with him to come home, as I honestly thought I was going crazy. However, logic put it down to being in a foreign country and alone with all the stress that we had been going through. I was missing Terry and felt I could not cope without him.

Terry came home and, as a thank you for taking me shopping and popping in to check on me, as well as his cows, we invited Bruno and Odile round for dinner. It really was time we got to know them.

I prepared a roast dinner, and after advising me on how to cook the chicken correctly, we settled down with a nice bottle of wine and enjoyed the smell of the smoke wafting from Bruno's Gitanes.

"The man who lived here before," I asked, "did he have a wife?"

"Yes," they replied.

"Did she kill herself?" I asked.

"Mais oui, how do you know?"

"Oh, I have had a lot of strange dreams since living here, she jumped off the cliffs at Granville didn't she?" I replied.

"Yes, that's right she did," they were beginning to look apprehensive.

"Was it because she was depressed because she could not have a baby?" I asked.

"That's right, all her sisters were able to, but she didn't fall pregnant and it made her very unhappy. Sometimes she would just blank you and you never knew what mood she would be in if you visited," interjected Odile.

They went on to explain that her husband came home one day to find her car gone and then the Gendarmes had contacted him to say a body had been found at the bottom of the cliffs – this had all happened the previous year.

Our neighbours went on to tell us that the husband had tried to stay and make a go of it, but with his wife dead, his heart wasn't in renovating the house any more. It seemed pointless to him and so he put it up for sale.

Great, we had not only upped sticks and moved to a foreign country, we had a ghost to contend with - this was going to be great fun I thought.

It wasn't until many years later that I found the papers relating to the purchase of our house and read them closely. By this time my French had improved dramatically and I could actually understand what was written on the deed of sale. I discovered that the woman who lived in our house committed suicide on the same day Terry and I got married, then a year later on our wedding anniversary we visited the house and agreed to buy it there and then. It had been the first anniversary of her death – a year to the day that she had killed herself.

From time to time she still visits – we will have nights of broken sleep. Some of our guests refuse to sleep in the attic bedroom. The dog will start barking at nothing, well, nothing that could be seen by human eyes. We always know when she is about, but at least she has stopped trying to persuade me to kill myself – so that is a good thing.

After another disturbed night we were in the kitchen having a late breakfast. With our interrupted night neither of us was on top form. She didn't just pick on me.

I whispered tiredly, "Just imagine this wasn't enough for her and she was French, so it is no wonder that I'm struggling with living here. I'm just not sure we will ever fit in, and I'm fed up with trying," I complained.

"Your right, it's not working out," Terry snarled tersely at me.

I nearly fell off my chair. Was he coming round to my way of thinking?

"I read your diary; it's not good isn't it? - I had no idea you were this fed up."

I had been trying to tell him.

"Perhaps we should split up?" He said exhaustedly.

Sex, Chelsea And Letting Go

Saturday May 1st

Sam had run off and come back filthy, I mean really filthy - in fact so dirty that after my initial disappointment and wanting to murder him, it was hilarious. I had to get a photo of this, so I got out my camera and captured his grubby image. After I had hosed him down, given him a nice shampooing; getting soaked myself into the bargain, I downloaded it to my Facebook page with the caption 'At least he came home'.

Later that night the comments came in -

Sophie: Oh my God, what happened?

Me: He ran away

Sarah: ahhh ahhhh the poor thing

Me: what do you mean poor thing, poor me, it was me who had to wash him

Annie: Why did he want to do that?

Me: Because he is a looney dog with a death wish

James: Oh that's our Sam!

Me: Don't you get encouraging him!

Karin: (my German friend) Ah he is so like his son

Me: You poor thing

Karin: I love them both, father and son

Me: Do you want him then.........?

Silence..............No more postings

Terry said the caption should have read 'free to good home' we will never know, there might have been some takers.

Not had a chance to talk about what we are going to do, it's been all go what with Joy and plans to go to Chelsea, I thinks it's going to have to be put on hold. Anyway the sun is shining and everything always looks much healthier at this time of year. We seem to have turned the corner at long last, we had the 'make up' sex so we're not calling the divorce lawyers and everything has been a lot calmer. Sometimes living here pushes you to the limits.

I had just read an article about an English couple in Brittany who after five years of trying to get their luxury golf hotel, spa off the ground, they had hit rock bottom. Broke and worn down by the French bureaucracy. The newspaper reported that he had phoned his neighbour to say he was about to commit suicide, he had explained he'd murdered his wife, set fire to her, then tried to hide her body in a builders sack by pouring concrete over her. He was now in custody, their child in care, wife dead, all because they dared to live the dream.

May 3rd

Sarah phoned. She suggested we meet up when I come to England to go to the Chelsea Flower Show. She also said that she would like to come back to France with me and stay for a week. She said she had sent off an application form for television's Deal or No Deal, a game show, hoping she could win enough money to get her through Uni and pay off her student loan. Why not, I replied and made a mental note to watch this programme as I had no idea what she was talking about.

She was just about to make some cupcakes, but she didn't have any eggs, so I suggested she made biscuits instead. She told me she preferred to nip down to the Hummingbird Bakery as nothing could beat their delicious red velvet cupcake. Said she was thinking about giving up smoking and wished she had never started, I couldn't help blaming myself for this.

When she and Ashley were little, I was living in North Devon and as I had to meet the mortgage payments on the business my ex-husband and I had bought, I rented out the flats to anyone who had the money. One of my lodgers was a lady called Sheila Tooley who had moved from West Bromwich to retire to the seaside with her huge dog, and as she had been unable to shake off her former

94

lodger, he had come too. I therefore rented them two separate flats.

I used to leave the children with Sheila, who looked a lot like Robin Williams when he played Mrs Doubtfire. She was a jolly old dear, in her sixties and with a delightful Birmingham accent. She had a monstrous Great Dane called Cilla and if you walked by her flat you would often hear her shouting

"Get down, Cilla, get down!" she had no control over that dog at all.

Anyway, she would often babysit for me, I think she liked to get away from the overpowering smell of the dog.

She was good with children and had a natural flair with them. It was like having your fairy godmother babysit. The only problem was that she was a chain-smoker, well I suppose it made the dog's smell bearable, and being on a pension and enterprising, she bought loose tobacco and rolled her own. She had a little machine, filter tips, the lot and she would keep the kids happy by getting them to roll her fags for her all night. Terry said she should have paid me as she was exploiting them, child labour and all that. He said that if they were living in Manila those kids would be on at least a pound a day.

Looking back, perhaps it was Sheila's habit that had got Sarah hooked, let's face it how many eight-year old girls can roll a perfect cigarette - that takes some skill. I think she was even selling them to the lodger - Sheila not Sarah. However, a few years later Sarah was nearly expelled from her very posh girls' school for selling packets of fags to her school friends, which she had bought whilst in France on her school holidays. I had to smile at the disciplinary letter I received from her headmistress, at least it showed her entrepreneurial spirit.

May 10th

Things to do:

Buy Sarah a cook book and Paul McKenna's CD on how to give up smoking

Mend Terry's work jeans

Buy a new lead for the dog

Card for Terry's birthday

Order Star Trek DVD's for Terry's birthday

Concrete the step outside the shed

Just got back from walking the dog and all was going well until he spotted some rabbits and that was it. He yanked himself free of the lead and sent me flying. Walked home alone nursing a bruised knee and vowed to take the bangers out with me when I exercise him next time.

How can a dog that is petrified of just about everything run off? You would think he would be too frightened to go anywhere. He really is some mixed up senseless animal. He is terrified of the dishwasher, especially when it changes cycle, the vacuum cleaner, my hairdryer, the microwave when it 'pings' and just about everything except, rather bizarrely, Terry's motorbike and the chainsaw. Terry says this proves he's a man's dog. You could have fooled me.

Alana and Les were over again, I realised when I spotted their Volvo parked in their drive. I knocked on the door but no one answered, well it was after lunch so they might have been having a siesta. Hopefully I will catch them before they go home. She had some original cartwheels outside her house and I wanted to know if they were for sale, as one would look attractive propped up outside our house.

Mum phoned to say that we have to go to Joy's flat when we go to Chelsea.

"There are still things to sort out before putting it up for sale," she said, "I've arranged for three estate agents to meet us, they just better show up on time, don't want to be hanging about all day."

After the last visit I knew she was dreading it, I could sense the apprehension in her voice when she said, "God knows what we're going to do there's still loads of stuff to move."

I said I didn't mind and would see if Sarah would also help, I didn't hold out much hope of that, but thought it sounded reassuring.

Mum would organize it all, she wasn't sure how we would manage it, but it had to be done and we had no choice. Mum said they had done a decent job before, but it was still a big mess. She was upset by the whole episode, so at least I would be able to give a little support.

She had been to see Gran, who was refusing to get out of bed and have her hair done. She said she would move when it warms up a bit, she has already missed two summers, so global warming had better hurry up or she will never make it.

Gran had seen Grandad that morning, but remains as cross as ever about his 'affair' and keeps going on about hearing Grandad and this other woman (still no name) having sex in the room above her head.

"What do you think about that our Karen? I'm fed up telling her he's dead."

I just didn't know how to answer her. Gran is sex mad and is convinced that some man will come in her room and have his wicked way with her in the night. I am not sure if this is a worry or wishful thinking. Well I suppose if Grandad is up to it, then she probably thinks she is missing out.

May 11th

Ashley and Sophie are home for the weekend, so I won't see much of Ashley. He seems to have a better sex life than I do.

Anyway, at least with the youngster's home it will give me the chance to find new recipes for variations on mashed potatoes, Sophie's favourite.

Sophie will finish her exams this summer and because she wants to go to University in England with Ashley she has decided to have a gap year, as Ashley has another year left. Sophie therefore has applied for a position in Ireland as an au pair for nine months, so I suppose they want to make the most of being together.

I just wish they would start taking their University applications seriously - everything is tomorrow with the young, when will they realise there is no tomorrow, only today.

You end up saying the same thing over and over - I can't work out who is worse, Ashley or her, but I have a good idea it is that lazy son of mine. That's what Guns 'n Roses should have called their song. Axel Rose and Slash obviously had not brought up teenagers when they wrote those lyrics.

I dread the day when Ashley leaves though, he taught me so much about heavy metal and French philosophy. Ashley even makes a lovely Victoria jam sponge cake that the Women's Institute would be proud of. What the hell will I do when he's gone? Who will boss me about in the kitchen and help me choose curtains?

I have to admit that once upon a time I wished he was gay - we even suspected it for a while - well, with all that baking and his enthusiastic interest in soft furnishings, it was a bit touch and go. You find homosexual men are ever so nice to their mums. It would have been pleasant, we could have carried on going shopping together and made scatter cushions whilst discussing Robbie Williams. But it wasn't to be; His girlfriend was creased up with laughter when he told her. If she ever has sons of her own I'm sure she will understand one day.

Terry said he didn't know what I was going on about, as when Ashley is at home all I do is complain about the mess or noise he makes. Or why he doesn't get round to doing his washing until nine o'clock on a Sunday night then expects it to be dry and ready for school the following day. When he is home there is mud all up the stairs because, on the rare occasions he does walk the dog, he leaves his muddy boots on. Usually, after he has trampled across a ploughed field, with Sam in tow.

Only last week I came back from shopping to find a note on the kitchen table that read:

MUM

IMPORTANT - READ THIS - BEWARE!

SAM HAS CAUGHT A BABY RABBIT, SO DON'T LET THE

HUNTER IN WITHOUT CHECKING HE HASN'T GOT IT!

DON'T TRY GETTING IT OFF HIM OR HE'LL GO MAD!!!

(Sorry if he's shown it to you already....)

Ash x

I went and knocked on his bedroom door as I hadn't seen anything and Ashley came downstairs asking if I had not noticed the blood all over the step. I said that I hadn't, but that the dog was in the kitchen and there was no sign of the rabbit. Ashley was relieved at this as apparently the dog had ripped the rabbits face off and he had left him mauling it outside. I felt quite sick at this, but said that he must have eaten it as there was no sign of it now, no fur or bones, nothing at all. Ashley thought that this was possible, as it was only a baby about the size of his fist.

The following day it was hard not to have a good look at his poo. I was curious at how an eaten rabbit would come out, would there be fur? After all, when he ate my sequined cushions his poo was sparkling for days.

When I told Sarah she screamed, "Oh mum, that dog is a killing machine! He's gross - you are going to have to do something with him, he's out of control."

What could I do? Shoot him?

May 12th

"Mum," Ashley shouted.

"What? What do you want?" I shouted back - living in a big house a lot of shouting goes on.

"Alana phoned; I said you were in the bath"

"Oh yeah, what did she want?" I shouted back.

"Well", said Ashley laughing, "she actually said that she would like to see that".

I had always felt that there was more to her big hands and feet that she was letting on.

"Did she say anything about that cartwheel?"

"Yeah, Les will drop it off this afternoon, fifty euros she wants for it"

"Bloody hell Ash, don't tell Terry the price - he will go mad. Still it will look nice outside the cottage," I gasped.

One of Terry's customers interrupted my mental calculations as to how much food I could have bought with it, as I quickly found fifty euros from my purse, and popped it on the dresser.

Christine had become good friends after one of her late husband's final requests was that his wife promised to have the back of their house rendered by Terry, as he trusted him and knew she would be in safe hands. We could hardly turn down a dying man's last wish for building work could we? We had never had such touching compliment and Terry had risen to the challenge and kept to his word, nothing was ever too much for this lovely lady.

We also had a lot in common, because she had recently acquired a dog. She was wondering if he could quote for a new potting shed she wanted erecting. We agreed to call over at the weekend, but I was not sure if we should take the dog this time.

The previous time we had visited, we tied Sam to a tree outside her house because she has several fish ponds and I just knew he would have careered into them splashing wildly like a mad thing, killing all the fish. Wolfgang had at least warned me about this.

I didn't want to be shown up, so while we had a nice cup of tea, he was safe in the shade of her sweet smelling old lilac bush, in the back garden. When I went to check he was okay I realised he had company, the little French poodle that lives next door had come calling. Now Sam is a big dog, but he is never aggressive to smaller dogs - even the really tiny ones. Anyway, the little poodle was underneath him and, as Sam was tied to the tree, he could not get away - the poodle had Sam cornered. To my horror I realised that the little poodle was licking energetically at Sam's private parts. Admittedly Sam didn't look like he minded too much, but when he saw me he became quite agitated, so I tried to get the poodle to let go and go home. However, the neighbour's dog was having none of it and just lapped harder at Sam's 'dog-hood'.

By this time Terry had heard the commotion and come out of the house to see what was going on. So too had the French next door neighbour who, totally ignoring his own dogs sexual misdemeanours, proceeded to start the questioning game. Trying to find out the usual 'who we were, where we lived, what we did' cross-examination the French are so fond of.

"Soo you liv in France ow long?" He started unable to take his eyes of my cleavage. Before I could answer he shot me another interrogation bullet, sidling up to me.

"Where's you come from hin ingland? France is nice oui? You looverley, sexy Engleesh you loves it ere" He carried on undaunted, now starting to up the flirtatious game he was playing, even more. I could see where his dog got it from.

I could sense Terry's unease at his banter, which he was trying to seduce me with, Terry was not having any of his Gallic charms. He informed the owner of the poodle that if he didn't remove his animal from our dog's private parts immediately and stop this dog rape, he would pull down the French mans trousers and show him what it felt like to be publicly humiliated. Needless to say he didn't hang about. I was most impressed, I had no idea that my husband knew so many French swear words, or would be prepared to go that far for our pet. He explained that James our new labourer, had taught him them.

Anyway, I didn't think it was fair to take Sam again, even if he had enjoyed it. It's not right taking your dog somewhere that he will be sexually violated, it's just wrong and I'm sure if the Kennel Club heard about it they would brand us as depraved parents.

May 24th

Terry's birthday!

Celebrated with a lie in, it is a Bank Holiday here today in France. In fact, there are so many Bank Holidays in May it is a wonder any work gets done at all. What with that and the two hour lunch break.

We have a good old laugh here about the Huit-a-Huit shop in the village as they open at nine, shut at twelve, re-open at two thirty and close at seven. I don't think 7/11 would get away with that. Ashley is off school too, so we decided to take Sam for a walk on the beach.

Terry declined to come as he said it was his birthday and he could do what he wanted, so he was going to sit in his cinema watching the Star Trek DVD's that I bought him and getting drunk. His idea of birthday heaven Jean Luc Piquard and a bottle of Famous grouse.

It was a lovely early summer day and, although it was a Bank Holiday, it was surprisingly quiet on the beach. We got out of the car and the dog smelt the sea - he loves water. He started to pull on his lead and I warned Ashley, who was holding him, to hang on tight. Sam was just too strong and he whipped Ashley round and launched into the sea, going further and further out.

We had chosen this beach as it was on the mud flats and dangerous for swimming because of the strong currents, so there would be no bathers to annoy. The idea was to let Sam have a paddle, not go body surfing over the waves. The tide was going out, and it was going out fast. All we could do was watch in horror as the dog disappeared further and further into the distance. I began to cry as I could see that he was not able to swim back to us and his head had started to go under the water.

There was a family with small children watching and they were crying hysterically that the animal was drowning and going to die. Eventually I could take it no longer and, despite the strong current, Ashley volunteered to rescue the dog. We made a chain with our jumpers, which enabled him to just reach Sam. He was relieved and held on to Ashley, and Ashley was able to pull him safely to shore, while I pulled both of them with our hastily constructed rescue line.

We reached the shore exhausted and wet through. We scrambled up the bank and sat there chilled to the bone and shaking. With trembling fingers I rolled Ashley a cigarette, handed it to him and told him I felt he deserved it. This was the first time I had acknowledged he smoked and had offered him a roll-up. Not only was my mad dog driving me crazy, he was undermining my parenting skills.

We still had to hold on to the dog, which was not at all perturbed by nearly dying and was ready for another go. So, after getting our breath back, we decided to head back to the car vowing never to bring him to the sea again.

As we walked back, past the family, we noticed that the small children had dried their tears and were recovering. They had enjoyed the excitement of the rescue and were now cheering and relieved to be giving Sam a pat and a hug. In typical Sam fashion, he just lay down and showed them his sandy stomach.

May 26th

Flew to England and Mum and Dad picked me up from East Midlands airport. I was going to catch the bus, but as I had to change in Leicester, I think my dad was worried I would not make it home at all, as there is a Primark right next to the bus station.

Off to the Chelsea flowers show tomorrow. Mum was all organised and knew where we were going, so I could sit back and relax. After we had arrived in Notting Hill and settled in to our hotel room we decided to pop down the road to get some milk, mum had bought her travel kettle with her.

A real result – we were unable to find a supermarket, but the local Marks and Spencer's not only had a great food hall, but it had just taken delivery of its latest summer clothes collection. So, in we went and I excitedly busied myself trying on loads of clothes whilst leaving Mum to go and find the milk.

I looked at my watch and realised it was coming up to six o'clock, so I asked mum to check with the assistant what time they closed as we really did need to get that milk. Ten pm was the reply. Wow! That's fantastic, I could spend all night in here. What on earth would they think of that in Normandy?

May 29th

Sarah picked us up from our hotel and drove us to Joy's flat, so at least we did not have to traipse all over London on public transport with my now heavy suitcase full of Marks & Spencer's underwear and clothes.

She left us there as she had a few jobs to do and said that she would pick us up later in the afternoon. With my mum still drooling over sighting Alan Titchmarsh (he's much taller than I thought- she said) we got stuck in.

The flat was bleak, dark and in need of renovation. I could not imagine living there. It was enough to send you mad, there was stuff everywhere. The estate agents turned up on time and in between their visits we were able to sort out a few things. It was at this stage that my mum realized there was no way her and Dad were going to be able to clear the flat on their own.

No one else in the family had the time or inclination to help - there was a lot of stuff, and when it comes down to it, disposing of someone else's life is not easy. Luckily mum had the telephone number for a removal guy. His mate had one of the garages behind my mums' house in Leicester and had given her Gingers card. She phoned him and, as luck would have it, he was in the area and could be with us in half an hour.

Ginger turned up and we agreed a price to clear the lot. This was a huge relief! The bed was still here on which she had died, there were stains on the mattress from her decomposing body. It was all really horrible and I am not ashamed to say, I was glad to get out of there. I just hoped my Mum would not have to go back again.

We had found a few note pads and jottings that were quite strange. They were the ramblings of a disordered mind consisting of chronicles on what would happen if she died. However there was nothing practical, just thoughts and reminders to brush her teeth, comb her hair and a fantasy diary of her ideal wedding - things that just didn't make sense to anyone else. She had obviously at some point been a very clever lady, it was hard to work out what had gone wrong and how she had ended up dead and finally alone.

Saturday May 30th

My ideal day, Leicester shopping with my Mum and daughter. I love it - we have a real good laugh. We always end up buying more than we need and then go home for a fashion show, showing my Dad all the bargains we have found, heaven!

Called into see my Gran in her care home on the way back. She had just had her tea and had managed to smear chocolate cake all over herself, but as we entered her room and saw her, chocolate cake was not the first thing we thought of.

After mum had cleaned her up and calmed her down, she was still furious that Grandad was not talking to her, we had a lovely time. I got her photo album out and we went through it, reminiscing about old times and the fun we'd had. Friday nights at the Bingo, then Gran and Grandad would take me for a Chinese; holidays in the sun and lazy summer days in my Gran's garden stealing the peas off the plants. Watching my dad fix the twin tub on the back yard and swearing with fury at it.

For a while now she has been telling all and sundry that Terry and I and must get married again, to each other thankfully. She is insistent that we have a 'proper wedding' with me wearing a white dress, lots of bridesmaids and Terry in a posh suit - the works. I don't know why she keeps talking about this. We had a lovely wedding and, after the wedding ceremony in the Registry Office, we had a Service of Blessing the next day with a handful of family and friends in the tiny church of St Matthew in the beautiful coastal village of Lee in North Devon.

That day we had walked from the pub to the Church, from the Church to the pub and then on to the hotel - all with the magnificent backdrop of the rugged cliffs and sea. It had been a wonderful day. Sarah had read a moving passage from the Bible, I'm not religious - just like to keep my hand in, and our good friend the drunken postman excelled himself with an amazing gift of fireworks, luckily managing not to set fire to himself.

The only sad bit was when I looked in the church and about a half a dozen people had not turned up. I couldn't work it out, because Terry's Mum and step-brother had made it all the way from Scotland, even surviving a plane touching down on their train's track, the taxi breaking down on the motorway, and eventually arriving at 3 am that morning. They had turned up, they had made it and so had my family from Leicester. Terry's family and friends from Yorkshire were there and so were my friends from London, so why no show from our local friends?

They had an assortment of excuses; child sick, couldn't afford the taxi, car broke down, had to work, too drunk from the night before etc. We later found out these so-called friends thought our marriage was a sham and gave it six months tops.

Anyway, not sure at all why Gran keeps talking about us, renewing our vows. Perhaps it is something she wished she had done, as marrying just after the war, she didn't get her big white wedding and my Gran was always one for getting dressed up. She invented the shopping trip to Leicester to get a new outfit, coming home and showing us what she had bought, we had just carried it on. We couldn't let her down by stopping the tradition could we?

As a child growing up in the seventies, it was bliss. We had loads of freedom to wander where we wanted to and, as there was hardly any traffic, the streets in which we played were safe and apart from; the rag and bone man and various traders calling and selling their wares; the fish and chip man on a Friday and the Corona pop man who would deliver fizzy drinks; the bread man with his Mothers Pride loaves; the milkman and Eric's ice cream van, the streets were a safe place to hang out.

We would sit for hours on the pavements playing and trying to balance on a pogo stick. I would take my cat in my doll's pram dressed in a bonnet and frilly frock up and down the path for hours. We would have stalls outside our houses selling our unwanted toys (and my Mum's Elvis records) to get some cash in time for the afternoon round of the ice cream man. Life was simple and even the three day week didn't throw us, the power cuts were times for candles and ghost stories, "Vote for Ted and spend four days in bed," my dad would sing.

There was a lot of joking when the lady over the road was pregnant yet again, she already had four little ones.

"It must have been all that time in bed with the electric off and no telly," my dad announced. I didn't have a clue what he meant as I still thought the stork brought the babies. I was happy, I played hockey for the school and was a whiz at athletics, and dreamt of Olympic fame.

There was always someone to play with and some mischief to get up to. Unfortunately this usually involved me hurting (not intentionally) or damaging (intentionally) my cousin Susan and her things. The worst misdemeanours were dropping a lump hammer on her head and drawing all over her brand new bright orange wellington boots with a biro, came a close second! Susan didn't seem to mind though and we would happily go off together to fetch her Dad a pack of ten Park Drive cigarettes from the corner shop or go carol singing and spending our money on a bag of chips at the end of the night.

This was not to last, and when I entered secondary school my innocent childhood was over. Everyone seemed so big and I had never encountered so many cruel stares in one room and they weren't all from the girls. I didn't know boys could be like this and I often found myself to be the butt of their jokes. I had grown up with my brother, uncles, cousins and kids on our street and that's a lot of boys. They had accepted me, even if I always ended up in goal. I had no idea that boys could be so cruel and nasty, girls yes - but boys! This was new and scary.

It was all about how you looked, what you wore, how much money you had and how clever you were. I was an ugly duckling who wore hand-made skirts and home-knitted jumpers and certainly didn't have any money or brains. I had two nicknames at school, 'German helmet' due to my hair style, which was supposed to be the height of sophistication and fashion, being a Purdie cut, which my hairstylist had failed to reproduce. The other, as my boobs would not stop growing, I was cheekily called Raquel. Think Raquel Welch in 2000BC,it had just done the rounds at the cinema. I think these nicknames were supposed to be a term of endearment but I didn't see it like that at the time!

The boys took the Mickey out of me. Luckily I could still run fast and this helped me get away and home quickly. I hated it and they seemed to hate me. Boys, girls, teachers – everyone. Except one girl and she became my best friend. We were inseparable, where I was the ugly, stupid kid she was the attractive and very clever one, the popular girl that everyone loved. I'm not sure why she wanted to hang about with me, but she did. She introduced me to Deep Purple, blue eye liner, how to flirt and Kate Bush. Then, out of the blue, her dad got a new job and they moved miles away. I was devastated - no one wanted to know me then. I was on my own. Looking back at the diary I wrote that summer I can still feel the anguish I felt at that time.

July 3rd 1980

"I don't get on at all with the others at school; they pick on me and generally go out of their way to make me look stupid. I hate it. I'm all alone. I have no one."

July 7th 1980

"I am an outsider and I feel awful, I'm breaking into their 'gang' and they don't want me. I can't help it, I wish I had a close friend, someone I could talk to, I feel like a freak."

July 8th 1980

"At school they keep talking about Tipper and his party, nobody mentions me or asks if I am going. I'm not invited and they don't want me to go."

July 10th 1980

"Finished school today for the summer holidays and had a good old push off, from what I thought were my friends. I walked out of school and came home, I would not cry in front of them."

I remember that time so vividly. I had the whole of the school holidays in front of me with no friends and the knowledge that I had to go back in September and face my tormenters. I thought my life was over.

Luckily my mum could see how unhappy I was and, knowing that I was lacking in confidence, she enrolled me in speech and drama lessons hoping this would help. I loved it. The theatre became my lifeline - I could lose myself playing someone else and also made new friends who didn't make my life a misery.

I eventually settled into secondary school life and it soon became apparent that I had an ally in my teacher. He was so young and good-looking and all the girls fancied him (so did a few of the boys!). We became great friends.

Looking back I realize now that his favouring me had a lot more to do with me personally than guiding me towards further education. We all loved him and fantasised about being his girlfriend. There was a television programme on at the time called Shoestring with Trevor Eve playing the character Eddie Shoestring, the sexy detective. Well, our teacher looked like him - moustache, corduroy trousers, and dodgy tank tops - the lot.

Even after we had left that school to go on to the upper school at fifteen, a group of us girls would go back to visit him and sometimes I would go alone. This continued and, shortly after I turned sixteen, I went on one of my regular after-school visits to see him.

This time was different though and he explained that we could have a better chat if we went back to his house. It would be no problem and he would drive me home, making sure I was in time for tea so my mum would not worry.

Well I was really curious - teachers were a bit like gods and I had never been into a teacher's home before, so I was looking forward to seeing what it was like. I had been in his car loads of times - you know that song by the Police Don't Stand so Close to Me - well that could have been written about me, that was my life. I am sure Sting must have been a teacher at our school. My teacher would often stop at the bus stop and give me a lift or take me home if it was raining, but this was different. We had never been alone together in private, there had always been other people about - I was entering new territory and I didn't have a clue.

We arrived at his house - a pretty little terraced cottage a few villages away from my own home, and went inside. It was neat and tidy, small and cosy, but before I could venture any further in, he grabbed hold of my arm, swung me round and kissed me long and hard. I didn't resist - I just could not believe it, why me? He was my teacher - what was he doing making out with ME? Surely he should have chosen one of the clever popular girls - there was enough of them and I'm sure half a dozen of them wouldn't have minded. I was the loner with no friends. But perhaps that was it - he knew I didn't have anyone to confide in.

When he finished kissing me he said, "Do you know how long I have wanted to do that?"

I had no idea, but I wasn't complaining. I had never kissed a grown man before and his moustache was quite tickly and exciting. He explained how he loved me and always had. He said when he first spotted me as a gangly teenager with bad dress sense that the boys picked on, he just wanted to protect me. He had, however, always been mindful of my age and so had never shown his feelings for me before, even though he had wanted to. He knew I was now sixteen and hoped I felt the same way. I didn't really know what to think – after all, it's not every day your fantasy comes true and you get to snog your hero.

I suppose nowadays you would say that he had been 'grooming' me. We didn't use words like grooming and paedophile then, but I think that was what he had been doing. I mean, what he did was wrong and he overstepped the mark, it's not right to fancy your pupils and wait until they are of age and then seduce them. They are hardly going to turn you down after hero worshipping you for years and years. I was putty in his hands and he must have known this.

Our relationship, if you can call it that, was way out of order and on a totally different footing. Today he would have been branded a pervert or sexual predator. But back then it was different, I wasn't complaining. I had never been the most popular girl at school. The boys favoured the petite, clever ones - not me with my buxom chest, sparrow legs, tom-boy ways and an IQ of a mouse. This was a new experience for me to be singled out by a grown man we all had adored. It was hard to take in that he saw me in this light, as I felt sure no one else did.

After our initial assignation many more were to follow and he never stopped telling me how special I was and how he loved me. Fortunately it never went any further than kissing and messing about. He told me he was taking his time, explaining that he wanted me to be ready. He introduced me to the Rolling Stones, salad dressing, D H Lawrence and lime pickle. He had a neat little vegetable patch (I didn't offer to weed it) and we would lie by the open fire talking, laughing and listening to his music. It was bliss, I felt so grown up and he certainly treated me like one. At last I had my special friend, even if it was a bit of a weird relationship. I had someone to confide in and talk to, but I knew it wouldn't last.

I would have given him the world, as he had rescued me from my loneliness and with this power I could face anything. I started to be more confident, more assured and I was no longer scared of the boys at school. That is all they were - stupid little boys. I was going out with a man and walking tall. With my new found confidence I was attracting admirers like flies. It's true, as they say, you wait ages for a bus to turn up and then out of nowhere three turn up at once.

That same summer I was to meet my first husband on holiday and fall madly in love with him. I was friends with another lad who took me to the cinema and another who had started writing to me after joining the army. I was Miss Popular for sure.

My Mum said I had to choose one boy and not encourage the rest. Having so many fellas hanging around was not a good idea she felt - what would the neighbours think? I thought it was a brilliant idea and was having the time of my life.

I told my friend, who had moved away when we were fourteen, all about my romance with our ex-teacher in my letters to her. She was the only one I could really confide in, as I had never told any of the other girls at school. Because of the way they were with me, they would have ripped me apart and made it sordid and wrong. In my heart, I knew it was sordid and wrong, so I didn't want to have it confirmed by their jealousy and sideways glances. I think my Mum thought he was helping me with my homework, I'm not sure, but she never told me I couldn't go and see him. What with him being respectable and all he got away with it. Anyway after really falling in love with my husband to be on holiday that year, I told my ex-teacher it was all over. I was quite relieved in a way, as I really didn't want to be in this relationship anymore – I had sort of worked out by now he was just using me.

Many years later my friend told me that where I had left off, she had picked up and had started a relationship with our ex-teacher, even going so far as to choosing a different University to be nearer him. She said they had gone the whole hog and she had fallen for him hook, line and sinker. She was completely besotted, so when he told her he was marrying someone else, a child psychologist, would you believe it, she nearly killed herself. He broke her heart and I had no idea at the time. We had continued to write to each other, but she had failed to mention she was having it off with him. She had omitted this nugget of information in her letters or visits. I couldn't believe it, how could you just miss out all that? I felt really deceived, I had confided everything to her, but she had kept her affair to herself. Perhaps, like me, she knew that deep down it was wrong but again, like me, she just couldn't help herself? Anyway, she eventually told me all about it, fifteen years later.

I felt I had a really lucky escape. In fact, that year I had two, the second one was quite scary. My hairdresser had an apprentice working for her, an eighteen-year old student and as I had my hair done we got chatting. I agreed to go back the following week so that he could practice his colouring skills and dye my hair purple. I was really excited, punk was in and although not a punk I liked to dress differently. My dad called me dolly mixture or sparrow legs, I was growing up and experimenting with my own style - purple hair would be the icing on the cake.

I turned up after school and it seemed to take hours to create my new look. So long in fact that everyone else went home and left the student and me alone. The owner had given him the keys and he locked us in so we would not be disturbed. At last my new look was complete and I was over the moon. Eagerly anticipating my gratitude, the apprentice unzipped his trousers, levering his manhood out of his grubby faded nylon underpants. I was shocked, to say the least. Firstly because I had thought he was gay - it was the seventies and in those days if you were a hairdresser it usually meant something. But mainly I was shocked at his erect penis sitting in a forest of ginger pubes - I had never seen ginger pubes before and was quite taken aback at how bright red they were. I couldn't help staring.

Anyway, after regaining my composure I told him I was very happy with my hair but there was no way on this planet I fancied him, stating I thought he was gay - he was a hairdresser after all and wore a silver bracelet and glasses. So I asked him if would please put his man thing away, unlock the door and let me go home. I added that if he failed to do that, I would tell my older cousins what he had done and they would kick his fucking teeth in. This seemed to do the trick and he let me out. Sadly I had to grow the purple out of my hair and change hairdressers - I simply couldn't risk going back there, not even for a free hair colour.

Building The World

Wednesday June 2nd

Back home in France and it is beautiful and bright, so Sarah is outside sunbathing, making the most of the warm weather, reading her Kindle. I had warned her to cover up because hearing Bruno's car on the drive I knew he had come to check on his cows. He would be so pleased to catch Sarah in her bikini (are all farmers sex mad?).

Sam seems content to see me home and welcomed yours truly by stealing the new cushions I had just bought. I asked Terry if the dog had behaved whilst I was away and he said that he had been no trouble at all. Bloody mutt - it must just be me he likes to wind up

Sarah asked if Alana was in France at the moment as she would love to see her. A few summers ago Sarah had decided that what we really needed in our garden was a pond, so armed with spades Sarah, Terry and I (Ashley was in bed) decided to dig one. We did really well and by tea-time we had excavated the hole. It was a scorching and very humid summer's day and as the first rumblings of thunder alerted our ear drums to the coming storm, Alana drew up in her dilapidated old Volvo. Looking like a cross between Cruella de Vil and Coco the clown, she had taken no prisoners in the fashion stakes that day. Reeking of cheap booze and, rather peculiarly, of a strong Camembert, at least that's what I thought I could detect.

"Oh how delightful, a pond," she slurred as Terry poured her a glass wine, while she attempted to roll one of her herbal cigarettes, spilling loose leaf tobacco everywhere. Then, without any warning, she ceremoniously fainted into the hole. As she came to Sarah and I helped her to a chair. Terry, not wanting to waste the wine, had quickly drunk it down and replaced it with the water that was gushing out of the hosepipe. It was obvious that she had consumed quite enough for one day. Concerned about her, we gathered around.

"I think it is the air pressure, there is a thunderstorm on the way and it made me giddy," she woozily explained.

"Oh, and I thought you were just shit-faced," retorted Terry.

After a lie down and nice cup of Earl Grey, she sped off up the drive taking most of our gravel with her, Just as the first drops of rain hit the sun parched earth.

Sunday June 6th

Said goodbye to Sarah at the airport, felt miserable and wished she was staying longer. Now she is older she no longer wants to spend all of her summer holidays with us as she has a life, lucky girl.

This is the best bit - the summer here is delightful with long lazy days and stunning blue skies. Sitting out at night watching the satellites pass by and the odd shooting star, with a decent bottle of wine that only cost three euros. It is a truly magnificent feeling.

Every year we promise to take two weeks holiday in August like all the sensible French Artisans, but for some reason it never works out and we always end up taking on work. We really do not have any choice, as there is no guarantee of consistent employment here, so you have to be prepared to pass up holiday times to finish that job, or make enough money to pay the inevitable bills that flood onto the doormat in September.

Most of our customers were like clockwork and will turn up February half-term, Easter holidays most of July, August and October half-term. Only the really hardy ones come for Christmas, but you can put money on them turning up at these times and sadly that's what it's all about. We cancel our holidays so we can quote them for work and get paid for what we have done. We just never end up having the time off ourselves. This year was going to be no exception, therefore while the children were away on holiday with their Father, somewhere warm and exotic, we would be working again.

Tuesday June 8th

Annie emailed me to say she is off on holiday next week with her girl friend. No luck on the man front - she had found a nice guy on the Internet dating site who sold fireplaces. It was good for a while, but after a few pokes in the hearth, she had kicked him into touch, he was just not the 'one'. So she was on the look out again, but I could tell, her heart wasn't in it and she was more than preoccupied with her son in Afghanistan.

I think she just didn't feel like having a good time with the thought of him out there. With the daily reports of Marines being killed and wounded, it is a dreadful time for any mother, sitting, waiting, jumping at every phone call, and every knock on the door. All of this didn't do anything for a carefree love life, not wanting to be caught with your knickers down having a good time. I don't think she would be able to forgive herself if anything happened to her son, her sex life would have to be postponed.

"It's bad enough going away on holiday," she sighed, "I don't think I'll be able to let my hair down."

"Don't be silly, get a couple of cocktails down your neck and you'll soon loosen up!" I said trying to inspire her, "you know what you're like when you've had sex on the beach and a long comfortable screw! Go and recharge your batteries. When Paul comes home in October you will be running around looking after him, up to your eyeballs in dirty washing, and feeding him up again."

I prayed he would come home safe. I wouldn't want anyone to have to go through the loss of a child, I knew most of all what that felt like, and you just never get over it.

Friday June 11th

Had to get up early and take Ashley and Sophie to Avranches, which is about forty minutes away, as they had to be at the Lycée for seven-thirty in the morning for their exams. Ashley had his French oral and Sophie her English oral. As we approached Avranches you could just make out through the morning mist, the haunting silhouette of Mont St Michel. I decided to wait for them in Avranches and spend some time walking around the Jardin des Plantes, enjoying the damp sickly smell of the lavander and wild sage as I appreciated the peace.

Sophie came out of her exam first and she was excited as it had gone well, the examiner even asked her if she had lived in England. The amount of time she spends at our house she might as well! I said it was probably all those films she and Ashley watch, well it wasn't talking to us at the dinner table.

Ever since Ashley had first met her and teased her for saying 'willy' instead of 'really', she was unsurprisingly very shy of speaking English. Sophie was prone to just nod or give monosyllabic answers. It had got to the point where we had given up on ever having a proper conversation. So when she came out of her exam gushing and talking English non stop I was slightly taken aback. She could obviously understand it all - I just had to convince her she could speak English in front of Terry and Ashley now.

Thursday June 17th

Ashley's school report arrived and he had been placed first in his class, he had done really well, gaining excellent grades for his baccalaureate next year. He should breeze through if he keeps this up. He said he was really looking forward to receiving his certificate next year and was thinking of turning up drunk with a fag in his mouth as his headmistress would not be able to say a thing. He was suspended a couple of years ago for drinking beer on his Wednesday afternoon off and also has been labelled a druggie although he assures me it was only rolling tobacco. It is amazing he is still at the school, and being able to gain such results was surely a testament to his capabilities. Unfortunately he still carried the stigma of being a foreigner and I feel that even if he got the top marks in the school, he would still be that long-haired English kid who will never amount to much.

Mum phoned to say that there was still loads to be done in sorting out Joy's estate. She had left a will, but it was not witnessed and is therefore not valid. There will now be a long process of finding all the benefactors, which could take some time. Mum is reluctant to go anywhere until it is all sorted and so has decided not to come to France this summer.

She had been to see Gran who was a bit tearful and not very coherent, preferring to talk about every one that was dead and believing them to still be alive. Her grip on reality was beginning to slip further away. She told mum she had been down the street that morning calling round to see her Mum and sister, then

116

popped up the chippy for some fish for her and Grandad, although he was not at home when she got back.

"Out with that woman again," she said.

"Ask her if she ever sees him in a purple shell suit or wearing a gold medallion?" I said.

"What on earth are you on about, Karen?" my mum replied.

"Oh nothing, it was a long time ago," I trailed off.

Wednesday June 23rd

Terry has picked up a lucrative job building a house for some English people, he had been recommended by their electrician. Apparently they had fallen out with the last builder due to his tendency to turn up drunk – that is if he bothered to turn up at all. It transpired he had also been helping himself to the building materials.

We went to have a look at the site, which is just at the concrete base stage. The only down side is that it is in 'dodge city' and there are so many cowboy builders here that you feel out of place without a Stetson on. The English have really taken over here and apparently if you go to the local supermarket it's hard to spot a French vehicle.

They told him they wanted it finished so that they could move in for Christmas. I invited them to come round for dinner so we could have a proper chat, knowing there is not a cat-in-hells chance of them moving in for the holidays, well not if they wanted a roof and walls. After an evening meal and an attempted reality check, we hadn't deterred them, and they were determined as ever to proceed with the build.

However Terry is starting to have real problems with this customer, the new build is coming along well, but the customer is now blanking him and not speaking to him. He can't work out what he has done wrong, as all he is doing is barking out his orders as he knows that they are desperate to get into the house for Christmas. As the customer doesn't have a clue, Terry has been pushing the build along.

"What on earth could I have done?" he asked me, "I'm the only one who seems to see any urgency. That bloke hasn't got an inkling and my labourer is just about as bad. It's like working at the circus with a couple of clowns bumbling around."

As I was having my hair done in the same area the next day, I said I would call past. Hopefully I could get to talk to the customer and find out what was going wrong, and alleviate the tension. This reminded me of a difficult customer we'd had once before where we had named her 'she who shall not be named' as we were fed up with saying her name. One of the labourers 'she who shall not be named' had employed to work with Terry, was called Tubby. Tubby was okay, he was a good worker and although he liked a drink he didn't have a problem with it, although he did have a tattoo on his penis that said HOT, which, he told us, was short for hold on tight. Apparently he had fallen asleep in a drunken stupor and a girlfriend had made her mark.

However the other labourer she had employed, Moz, was a bit of a handful to say the least. Moz was also staying with 'she who shall not be named' as she had flown him over from Italy. The trouble was that Moz really liked a drink and, after drinking her house dry, 'she who shall not be named' and Moz had fallen out. Not wanting to slow the job down and in need of a labourer Terry invited Moz to live with us for the duration of the project.

He was like a whirlwind and took over our house and our lives. He knew everything, well he was half French, he insisted on doing ALL the cooking, the shopping, arranged our entertainment, television was the devil's work in his opinion, Ashley's fitness - rugby lessons every night after school, Sarah's musical tastes - he had recorded an album and he proceeded to turn Terry into an ally in the drinking stakes, this did not take much. He was all over us like a rash.

The final straw came when, in the early hours of one morning, I caught him trying to persuade Terry into leaving me and them getting a place together. He wasn't gay, just a hopeless drunk who needed a sidekick to enjoy it and Terry was well up for that job.

Luckily the next week his beautiful Italian girlfriend arrived. She was as demure as he was brash, she was as polite as he was rude and she was as sober as he was drunk. She was exquisite and we could not understand what the hell she saw in him.

He had taken to dressing in an outrageous kilt he had bought, I had been dispatched with him to the Irish shop in Granville to help him find a skirt in his family tartan to surprise his girlfriend when she arrived. It not only surprised his girlfriend, but he got a right ticking off for insulting his father's family for wearing the tartan so disrespectfully when he visited them one weekend.

She was to stay for two months and, as she was an artist she wanted to carry on working. Terry therefore converted the end of the barn into a makeshift studio and we moved them into our gîte, so it all became a lot less stressed. We had our privacy and I had my husband back, although I'm not sure Terry was that convinced, he had enjoyed all that male bonding. I just put it down to alcohol withdrawal.

Finally the work was completed for 'she who shall not be named' and Moz and Maria had to return to Umbria. As we had always wanted to visit Rome and my fortieth birthday was looming, ever the Yorkshire man, Terry thought he could kill two birds with one stone - a holiday and birthday present. So we agreed to give them a lift back and enjoy a road trip to Italy.

Stopping off in Geneva to see Moz's sister and then we went on to Milan to stay with his friend, who danced at the Scala. He really was a living Billy Elliot but said that he was getting too old for it and the ballerinas nowadays were too fat to lift. He loved Milan, but was homesick for Bootle. However he had signed a contract to dance at the Scala until he was sixty-five, so Liverpool would have to wait.

We had another detour before we would finally arrive, as Maria had to meet one of her gallery owners. He had suggested we had pizza by the lake and as he was paying for us all, we could hardly protest. He delighted us with stories of how he was absolutely worn out as he had four mistresses on the go and a different mobile phone for each of them, even his wife. The stereotypical Italian was alive and well, selling Maria's paintings of 'nudes and pots' in his up-market tourist gallery near Trasimino Lake.

When we eventually arrived in Umbria we were not disappointed, set in the hillside a stone's throw from Assisi it was breathtakingly beautiful. Maria showed us around her home village and surrounding towns, pointing out frescoes and significant architecture,

We lapped it up, keen to see all the sights and get a real taste of Italy, even if that meant chauffeuring Moz in his ancient Jaguar around the area. We visited Maria in her studio, who was trying to dodge her maestro who had taught her everything about her craft and now would not be content until he had sold all of her work. He was causing considerable problems for her with his 'if it hadn't been for me' attitude. No wonder she had wanted to come to France for two months and I now suspected Moz was putting out feelers to get away from this man and the hold he had over her. It was like being in an episode of The Sopranos, only with more wine and pizza.

Like Sheryl Crowe we spent three days in Rome and had a wonderful time. I really relished the guided tour of the Coliseum complete with ancient Roman graffiti. It was pointed out that the painted phallus on the wall was to indicate where to obtain a prostitute, whilst enjoying the thrills of the gladiators. I couldn't help thinking about all the starving people in the world however when we experienced the exuberant decadence of the Vatican City.

It reminded me of a friend who had lived in Ireland as a child had once told me how on a Friday night, the local catholic priest would do the rounds collecting from the workers who had returned home wearily, with their pay packets in their hand and ask for a contribution to the church. This friend told me his mother had six children under nine and could hardly make ends meet. The kids having to share shoes to be able to attend school and this greedy priest would happily take their money.

We caught the train back to Maria's house worn out, only to be told they were having a party in our honour, so vast amounts of alcohol were purchased from Euro Cash and Maria taught me to make traditional bruschetta for the guests.

The rest of the party was a bit of a blur, but by the state of the place the next day I think we all had a good time. Especially Moz, who was asleep on the floor still in his kilt, curled up with the remains of a bottle of whisky and the cat.

We left Moz and Maria in Italy and made our way home. It had certainly been a birthday to remember and I really had had a fantastic time. I could not have enjoyed it more and felt that we had experienced a real taste of Italy and Italians - you don't get that from package tours.

Thursday June 24th

Had my hair done and called in to see what was going on at the new building site and find out if the customer yet. When I arrived Terry was up the scaffolding, with his labourer passing concrete blocks to him. The customer was sitting all alone trying to screw some bolts into oak pillars, so I sat down with him. It was obvious that something was wrong and I had never seen a client sulk before. I soon got to the bottom of it - Terry had asked him to cut some wood at the weekend and when Terry had arrived on Monday morning he had measured the wood. He had taken offence at Terry doing this - especially as Terry had told him that some of the measurements were out.

"I don't mind being corrected, but I don't like being made to look stupid," he told me.

Ah we were getting somewhere, I explained that, as they wanted to be in their house by Christmas, Terry was just trying his best to motivate everyone to get the work done. However, it did have to be done accurately. I explained that Terry was a bit of a task-master and did work hard, expecting anyone who was working with him to keep up. As he had wanted to work alongside him he was therefore required to step up to the mark and be prepared to be ordered about. All this was said in the nicest possible way, they were paying our wages after all.

I lightened the tone then and his wife turned up with his corned beef and piccalilli sandwiches, so we had a chat and she reminded me that they needed to move out of their rented accommodation by Christmas. I'm not sure why she was telling me all of this, I thought, she should be talking to her husband.

It is a mystery to us that customers just don't have a clue. Why would you want to build a house if you couldn't even cut a bit of wood straight and then, to top it all, just take no notice of any advice you are given. It is no wonder that people run out of money and end up going back to the UK, they are sunk before they have started.

Mind you, I managed to get a bed and almost new mattress for Ashley's room for twenty euros today from a 'returning to England - everything must go' advert on the Internet, so I really shouldn't complain. One person's loss is another's gain, as they say.

Sometimes you cannot resist checking out what they have when you go round to quote for work, because you just know that in about two and half years time they will be selling it all off to raise the money for the ferry tickets to get them back to England. Anyway let's just hope the tantrum is over and they manage to get some work done.

Wednesday June 30th

Still no change, Terry is still having difficulties with the client. He says that the atmosphere is awful and just does not know what to do about it. This was fast becoming a 'she who will not be named' situation and the topic of conversation every night was the same.

Eventually I asked Terry what exactly he had been employed to do. He was to turn up, do his work and get paid. However, as Terry was the only Artisan on site and the only one who had a clue how to build a house, he had taken it upon himself to also become the site manager, knowing there was a tight schedule.

"Herein lies the problem," I said, "you've overstepped the mark. He employed you to work for him, but he's in charge and you turn up shouting the odds, directing the build and he doesn't like it. You've undermined his position." I explained.

"But that's just silly, if I don't do that, then who will make the decisions and keep the build moving?"

"It's not your problem - you have to step back and let him get on with it. If he asks for advice so be it, but ultimately you have to doff your cap and nod your head - you are just the hired help."

Thursday 31st June

The sound has gone on the old telly, so we decided to go shopping and buy a new one. There is only one problem - you have to have a degree to operate it. I hope I get used to it, as after years of having Sky, we are now on Freesat and I have to re-learn everything. I hate it when everything changes, it's like my computer - I just get used to it then MSN has to upgrade itself and I don't know where I am for a month until I get my head around it.

I know I am a technophobe, but it really does my head in - I don't even have a mobile phone. I had one years ago, but got fed up with people disturbing me all the time, so when I moved to France I gave it up.

Last time I was in England I went into an Indian restaurant and asked if they had a pay phone, the waiter said "Why, have you had your mobile stolen?"

"No," I had replied "I don't have one."

"Where on earth do you live?" he asked me.

"France," I replied.

At least the customers could only phone the landline it was bad enough receiving calls at eleven at night and Sunday mornings. Imagine if I handed out a mobile number there would be no respite.

Anyway this job was paying well despite all the aggravation so I begged Terry to take a step back and just turn up and do what the customer wanted with no back chat about what a numpty he was. We had bills to pay!

Dad's, Dogs And Diaries

July 5th

Sam has a liking for my new cushions with sequins on, and to date, he has ruined three in less than a fortnight. The only one left has the beads literally hanging on by a thread - I could kill him. It wasn't until we had owned Sam for over a year that Wolfgang, Brigitte and Jenny (Sam's estranged doggy-wife) paid a visit and we told him about Sam killing one of my brother's kittens and a baby rabbit.

"Yes, he does that," Wolfgang said, "he had a reputation in the village where we live in Germany for killing cats, stealing chickens and raiding our neighbours' fishponds. Once he was even reported to be running through the streets with a goose in his mouth." Wolfgang continued, "when we moved to our new house in Germany, the man next door had three cats - he doesn't anymore."

Now you tell me, I thought, as I poured Wolfgang another glass of German wine. It was becoming increasingly obvious why Sam had been kicked out. As Jenny and Sam became reacquainted, mainly by sniffing each others bums, we chatted. They had brought his Kennel Club papers with him. They had bred from him and had three litters - I bet those puppies have got some issues carrying his genes. I thought to myself. At last we found out his official Kennel Club name. He is Golden Xanos von der Berkanalle! What a name, I tried it out on him and no response, it was just plain Sam to him. I think they must have bred him for his looks, as it certainly wasn't for his brain.

Wolgang asked me if I had heard of 'dinner for one' which is a New Year's Eve tradition in Germany. This strange British production is played over and over again in Germany on New Year's Eve or Saint Sylvester as they call it. We told him we had never heard of it - apparently it's a butler serving dinner for one - no other guests, I didn't quite get it, I just could not understand why they would want to watch that on New Year's Eve. I said to Terry I thought since the Berlin wall had come down, you'd like to think they would have some decent television programs now.

July 10th

Sarah phoned to excitedly let me know that Take That are getting back together.

"I know, I heard it on the radio this morning - I nearly wet myself! We just have to go and see Robbie," I cried.

Took Sam for a walk fantasising about seeing Take That in concert. I made a mental note that I must go on a diet - a concert could be announced at any moment and I need to look my best.

Mum phoned, "Take That are getting back together again!" she shouted excitedly.

"I know," I replied.

They had just got home from shopping in Leicester. Dad had seen a coat he fancied, so Mum gave him the money I had sent him for his birthday.

"His birthday is not for another week, but he liked the look of it," she explained, "he's so hard to please, and faffs around, so I thought, why not it gets it all over with."

Great - thanks for spoiling the surprise. I had asked her to get a garden voucher for him. I suppose she just couldn't face my Dad dithering about B&Q choosing something and I could hardly blame her.

July 21st

Mum phoned in a state - Dad had been rushed into hospital. My heart sank. He had suffered a heart attack about six years ago and, although he had made a good recovery, you just always worry it might happen again. I know I did, so goodness knows how my Dad coped. I think for the first year he thought he would die any day, so it was a really depressing time for him and it took a long while for him to calm down, relax and learn to look forward to things again.

My Dad is one of the funniest men I have ever met, he has a really good sense of humour and, as children, we would look forward to him coming home each evening from work and telling us his latest joke. We didn't have the internet in those days, but somehow he would churn them out and tell a different one every teatime.

My Dad is very likeable and everyone loves him. When he was young he was quite the handsome man about town. He played football, once famously scoring all four goals in a cup game, one of them with his hand – this was years before Maradona's 'hand of God'. He had been in the RAF and, after five years in the Middle East, returned home toned and tanned.

How could my Mum resist him? She was putty in his hands and, following a whirlwind romance, they had married. Or, as my Mum tells the story, she turned up at the bus stop to go to Coventry Palladium on an evening out organised by my Dad and asked the girl who was also waiting at the bus stop who her date was.

"George Bates," she had replied.

That would make sense, my Mum thought and vowed not to speak to the two- timing rat. He later explained he had only asked the other girl to be his date to make the numbers up on the coach. That's my Dad. He is an insatiable flirt and drinker, so everyone loves him. He is also one of the craftiest men I have ever known. He would run a book stall every year at the local carnival, my brother and I would be dispatched in June to collect for his stand, armed with a written cardboard note from my dad and my dolls pram, sometimes with my cat in it dressed up for the occasion in my dolls' clothes. My brother and I would go round the local streets knocking on doors and asking for contributions. Year after year he tirelessly sorted the books and ran that stall, I was so proud of his community spirit and commitment to our village.

"Dad, you work so hard every year with the book stall, wouldn't you prefer to have a rest?" I asked him one year.

"What and have nothing to read on my holidays, why do you think I do it? I get first picks on the good stuff, doesn't cost me a penny."

That's my Dad through and through - why pay for it if you can borrow or acquire it first.

Anyway, Mum calmly explained that it wasn't a heart attack, but that he had suffered a burst ulcer and it had literally exploded in the middle of the night, going all over the carpet, curtains and the bed linen. Apparently he had made a right mess

"But is he OK? " I asked.

"Yes he is fine now and says he feels much better after getting all that out," she replied.

They had called their Doctor, who told them to call an ambulance and get him into hospital. So after spending the rest of the night in a corridor. Mum had caught the bus home and was contemplating decorating the bedroom.

"Just goes to show it was a good job he bought that coat, he wouldn't be able to get to the garden centre now and it's his birthday tomorrow." Good old Mum - she always knows how to look on the bright side.

Phoned Sarah to tell her about Dad and she was beside herself, really upset and just wanted to jump in her car and go and see him. I reassured her that he was okay, it was not that serious and that he was ok. I said I would call her with any news and promised that he was fine. I got off the phone and had a good cry. Sometimes it is so hard being brave when you are so far away.

July 22nd

Dad's birthday and Mum phoned to say he was doing well. She had phoned the hospital and was going to see him this afternoon. There was even talk of him coming home today.

Later, Dad phoned to let me know that he was home. He said he felt fine, in fact he felt a bit of a fraud as he really was okay and had caused such a fuss. Anyway, he was taking it easy and enjoying the rest of his birthday. Mum had got the decorating books out as they would need a complete re-decoration. Apparently, it had been like something from The Exorcist and he had made a good old mess, she had even had to cut part of the carpet out as it was so bad. Poor old Dad. "Your mothers happy, never been keen on them curtains since we put them up," Dad said.

Friday July 23rd

Ashley and Sophie are off to England and I am taking them to the airport later. They are going on holiday with Ashley's Dad and are also going to look at some universities in England. I hope this spurs them on to do their personal statements and get organized. If they ever get to university it will be a miracle.

Sarah phoned, she was very upset as she has failed one of her compulsory modules in her second year at Uni.

"How did that happen?" I asked her, "It's all that work you are doing to pay your rent, you must have been working too hard."

"No mum, I failed because I didn't do enough work."

"Well what have you been up to?" I asked.

"Watching daytime TV mainly," she said, "and sleeping."

At least she knew where she had gone wrong, no wonder she had applied to go on Deal or no Deal, she certainly had plenty of time to study the rules. If she did get on the programme at least this would stand her in good stead.

I told Ashley about it all on the way to the airport. So not only do you have to get in to university, you have to turn up, I warned him. I despair, if they ever get anywhere I will eat my hat.

Drove home looking forward to a month on our own - just me, Terry and the dog. I was going to enjoy this, I had waited a long time to have so much time without the children. Things were improving on the divorce front, well it had been thirteen years.

The weather was perfect we were getting paid, on a regular bases and for the first time, for a very long time, life was good. We were joyful and content, had we finally turned the corner? I had put all the ideas of moving back to England out of my head, I really did think at last we were getting somewhere. Life in Normandy was on the up.

July 27th

Had the most awful day and night. Sam had run off yesterday and after an extensive search for him I was not able to find him. This was a first, I mean he has run off many times before, but he eventually came home. On this occasion there was no sign of him. As soon as Terry came home from work we went out looking again – nothing, not a trace. I asked my neighbours, but no one had seen him. Bruno told me that he had spotted him in the garden that morning when he was checking on his cows, he said hello to him and patted him on the head, so it must have been after lunch that he had gone off and just vanished into thin air.

I had a sleepless night again and awoke early. Terry and his labourer, James, offered to go and search for him again, but as they were working for the sulky client who didn't like to be bossed around, I said they better get going or he would be on the phone demanding to know what they were playing at.

I went out again in my car, nothing. Beside myself, I did not know what to do. So I phoned my mum. "Sam has disappeared," I cried, "he's been gone since yesterday afternoon and I have looked everywhere, been to all his usual spots, and looked in the ditches. I just don't know what to do," I sobbed. "Terry says he is probably lying dead at the side of the road somewhere."

"Calm down," my Mum said reassuringly "the best thing you can do is to put posters up, go to the vets and the Gendarmerie to see if anyone has found him. He is micro chipped and they have your address, so don't panic. I'm sure it will be alright."

I put the phone down and found a photo of Sam made a 'lost dog' poster and photocopied it a dozen times. I then sped off in my car, everywhere would be shut until two o'clock, but the bakers would be open, so after stopping to put my first 'Perdu: Sam' poster up on the gate at the end of our road, I carried on to the Boulangerie. As soon as I walked in with the poster in my hand and she saw Sam's handsome face, the owner asked if I had lost a dog. I said I had and she gave me a slip of paper with the name and address of a man a couple of villages away. He had come in to the Boulangerie last night to say he had found a Golden Retriever wandering along the main road, filthy, exhausted and looking like he had been in the river - this definitely sounded like my Sam.

I got into my car and, after glancing briefly at the note, sped off in the direction of the man's house. I knew the village and there were not that many houses. Not having a mobile phone and not wanting to waste time I decided to go straight there without phoning for directions first, I was just so anxious to see Sam alive and well. I didn't want to believe he might be dead or injured, but at some point this dog would have used up all his luck. It was getting scarier each time he did something stupid, he had managed to get away with it again, but how many more times will he be so lucky?

I got to the village, and although small, I could not find the house so I knocked on a few doors and eventually found someone at home, a charming old couple, said they knew who I was looking for. "Oh, the dirty dog, yes we know where he is," and they ushered me inside.

However, before they would divulge his whereabouts, I had to go through the usual question and answer game the Normans are so fond of 'Where do you live? How long have you been there? Are you married? What does your husband do? Does he have much work, where does he work? Do you have children? How old are they? Where do they go to school? Where exactly did you say you lived? Is that near Philippe Le Boucher's farm or are you near to Bruno Le Monnier?'

My patience was running out and I just wanted to scream at this point, 'PLEASE TELL ME WHERE I CAN FIND MY FUCKING DOG!'

At last I had parted with enough information to appease them and they released me, giving me directions to the house opposite theirs. I ran up the drive and there he was, tied up (a wise move) and looking deceptively clean and well behaved. I called out his name and Sam's saviour appeared.

"So that is his name, Sam," his rescuer said.

"Yes, yes and thank you so much for finding him and looking after him so well. I really appreciate your kindness," I replied in my best French.

"I found him on the road to Granville. He was filthy and worn out and looked like he had been swimming in the river, so I put him in the car and brought him home. I had to wash him as he was so dirty and I fed him."

I was so tempted to ask if he wanted to keep him as he had obviously taken a lot of time and effort to look after him. Anyway, I thanked him again but in my excitement I had not opened the boot to the car, so while I fiddled about with the key fob, Sam sat down in the biggest and muddiest puddle he could find and waited to go home.

July 28th

Ashley phoned today to say they had been to see The University of East Anglia and that they were impressed, both making it their number one choice. However, Birmingham was also in the running - being the home of heavy metal. The course at East Anglia is the best one for Sophie and Ashley is that laid back he would go anywhere. When we were in the process of choosing Universities for him to visit, I asked him "So where do you prefer?"

"I don't care really as long as I can go, I would be quite happy if someone said you are going to this Uni, turn up on this day, doing this course, sorted," he responded.

Had an email from Annie who said she was thinking of having a welcome home, belated twenty-first birthday party for her son Paul, who was due home from Afghanistan in early October. This was obviously her way of passing the time by doing something like arranging a celebration as she could put all her energies into that and not have to think too much about what he was going through out there. I emailed her back saying we hoped to be there and did she want some wine? Silly question.

Bought a mobile phone! It might take some time to work out how to use it, but I thought it was a good idea for keeping in touch with the children, a text is a lot cheaper for Sarah, so I can text her and we can talk for free on Skype. It will work out more cost-effective in the end, well that's what I told Terry.

Thursday July 29th

I decided that with Ashley away and Terry at work I would have a mammoth clear out. I would go through all our old papers and out of date guarantees and burn the lot, I love a good clear out - it feels cathartic to me and I can always think more clearly when the kitchen cupboards have been turned out.

I'm also fond of a good bonfire. My brother is horrified by this and tells me I will pollute the atmosphere. I asked him if he had seen the fireworks on Bastille Day - I didn't think my little fire would amount to much. He replied with "Well that's just typical, people like you don't care. You're all me, me, me - you just wait, one day it will be too late, after all those plastic fumes have gone up into the atmosphere."

He would rant at me and of course he's right. In an ideal world I wouldn't do it, but you know it's as if I can't help myself - I just love having bonfires, I'm also very fond of lighting the wood burner in the house and get quite territorial about it. I said to Terry that I thought in a previous life I must have been the servant girl who lit all the fires in the big houses or perhaps just an arsonist.

While I was rummaging through the piles of rubbish that we seem to collect in our lives (where does it all come from?), I couldn't resist reading my old diaries from when I was fifteen, so I put the kettle on and decided to have a good laugh.

It seems as if I spent most of my time worrying about my weight and what I looked like and what boys thought about me, that and watching Top of the Pops and Tiswas. I had attended my weekly speech and drama classes, endlessly performing in some play or other, or dragging anyone I could find to come with me to the Theatre. Along with Kate Bush, the Theatre was my life and I loved it, I planned to become a famous actress and had it all worked out. I was also amazed to read how well my brother and I got on, I know we had been friends, but we seemed to go everywhere together having similar friends and interests. It's amazing to think that I then left home at seventeen and a few years later he went to live in Holland.

I asked him recently why he thought we had both left the village where we had been brought up. It was unusual as most of my family is still there or very close by. He said he didn't know, but it just felt like the right thing to do at that time. He was trying to escape a failed love affair and I had also left because of a similar relationship. I had met a boy on holiday and, after years of writing and visits, I finally upped sticks and moved in with his Mum and Dad prior to us buying a flat of our own. I was a homeowner and married by the time I was nineteen, and working for the government in one of their prisons. Looking back, I can hardly believe I did it but I suppose at that age you just want a change of scenery.

I was happy and enjoying my new life, but it didn't last for long and sadly my first husband and I split up. We had just grown up and grown apart. I was a real little madam in those days and I needed a strong man to curb me or I had a tendency to walk all over them. My first husband was too nice, he was one of the good guys and didn't stand a chance, as I bulldozed through his life. He could not contain me and I was a lousy wife, not ready for the job so we fell apart. It was such a shame as he was a great person, funny and educated with great taste in clothes and music. He introduced me to science fiction, motor bikes and Frank Zappa and for that I will be forever grateful, as this was to come in very handy all those years later when I met Terry.

I never did go back to live in Leicestershire, but I could have, I was single and had thirteen thousand pounds from the sale of our flat. I was only twenty and could have got a transfer to a government posting. I didn't even think about going back, it just didn't cross my mind. I had made the break and I was not going to run home at the first sign of something going wrong.

Looking back I wished I had, I wished that I had found the courage to follow my dreams. I was still young, I could have applied to drama school and actually gone this time instead of working for the government, it wasn't too late. Somehow though, I just carried on doing what I was doing and my dream slipped so far away that it would always be just that, a dream.

I was brought up in the Midlands, but it is still quite northern and working class and I felt that acting was "not for the likes of us". – We weren't like that. Now, of course, I see how stupid that was as Julie Walters, Cathy Burke and the like were breaking through the barriers. You no longer had to be stick thin and beautiful to be a good actress - talent counted. I, however, was so short-sighted and so naive in thinking you had to be Helen Mirren to get into stage school.

My fame was to be put on hold forever. I had a different path to take - the dreams I had as a child were no more and I relegated them to the back of my mind. So as I sat sipping my cold coffee, a longing for my old self returned and I couldn't help wondering if there was more to life than what I had. The kids were grown up, nearly off my hands, so what would I do with the rest of my life?

Stagnate in Normandy? I didn't visit the Theatre anymore and I used to love that, we didn't even go to the cinema (the dubbing can be quite off putting), we didn't even have a local pub to frequent. My mum belonged to all manner of societies and committees, she and Dad were forever off here and there. I love my garden and my dog, and my husband come to think of it – but I wanted more – these simple pleasure were not enough for me. I was beginning to feel stifled even claustrophobic, it felt like I was standing on a railway platform and as the trains whizzed by. That was I pictured my life, and I was being left behind standing still.

Emails I Would Sooner Not Receive

August 1st

Had an email from Sarah asking me if I would like to send her some money so that when the Take That tickets come out, we will be able to get them straight away. After all, it was just a matter of time before they announced an album and a tour. I really must start taking this diet seriously - I don't want Robbie thinking I have let myself go. I decided to phone her, as we had not spoken for about a week, I had also seen an X-ray of her bearded dragon on Facebook and it seemed to have some sort of foreign object inside it.

She said she was sorry she had not been in touch for a while, but they had been having a terrible time, as it had been touch and go with Slash (the bearded dragon), and they were not sure if he would make it through his operation. He had eaten his thermometer and had to be rushed to the vets, where an emergency operation was performed. Sarah was now nursing him back to health - she will make such a good mum.

I asked James to show me how to find out how much credit I had left on my phone, as I couldn't work out how to do it. Terry asked me, why hadn't I looked at the instructions and I said I hadn't thought of that.

August 3rd

It's a lovely summer's day, so I decided to take the dog for a walk and go down to the stream to let him cool off. An hour later, I was sitting at home with my feet in a bowl of cold water waiting for the dog to return after chasing him over several fields and streams. As usual, I had returned home totally exhausted, let's hope the dog does the same or he will be grounded for the next month.

Phoned Sarah to see how Slash was doing.

"He is great, doing really well and is eating his food, but hasn't done a poo yet. If he hasn't done one by tomorrow I will take him back to the vet to see if he is okay," she explained.

That's a relief, as I don't think we could have coped with another bereavement in the family at the moment, everyone is still feeling a bit down following Joy's death. Ashley and Sophie are off on holiday with her parents for a week's camping in southern France. I have to get up and meet her mum and dad at six o'clock in the morning in Granville so they can make an early start. At least it will be light. Must get an early night in and leave off the wine.

August 4th

Got up at 5 am and woke Ashley. Had a coffee and told Ash to call Sophie, as she was supposed to call us to let us know they had left so we could rendezvous on time. She answered and was still in bed, lucky thing. No one in the house had woken up, but she would go and see what was happening.

She phoned back to say that her mum had told her to go back to bed. Sophie had explained that she thought they were having an early start and meeting us at six. This did not go down well and she was told to go and start packing up the car. She said she would call later with news of their departure. Ashley and I settled down to watch night-time TV and the omnibus of Coronation Street - who would think it would be on in the wee small hours of the morning.

Three cups of coffee, about ten fags and three episodes of Corrie later, Sophie called, everyone was up, there were five kids to get ready and hopefully they would be leaving at about half past seven, an hour after we were originally supposed to meet and as they lived an hour and a half away it would end up being two and a half hours after the arranged time. I could have stayed in bed until seven! I was fuming. Anyway, we were having fun and Corrie was really hotting up - at this rate we would be able to watch the whole week's worth.

Ashley called Sophie and she told him they were in the car and just about to leave. It was eight o'clock by now, so we would have to leave at nine to be on time. In the end they were three hours late, it must have been a record for Sophie's mum, although I later found out, they had once been so late for a weekend away that they gave up trying to get ready and just stayed at home. I can only hope that they start packing mid-week, they then should have a chance of getting home on time. You have to love the Normans, they would never cope in England.

August 6th

Started on the roof at last and as soon as we did, the heavens opened. Typical Normandy weather - you wait all year to do a job and the one week you choose to take off to do the roof, there are gale force winds and rain. I should have known, after all it is the most expensive time to visit, with the holidaymakers paying a premium for the summer holidays.

August 9th

Sarah phoned to let me know they had just had the vet's bill for Slash – five hundred pounds! They were not sure how they would pay it, but it might have to be a 'bank of Dad' job. At least Slash had now had managed to open his bowels. Wonder if I will get my 'Take That' tickets.

The roof is just about completed and Ashley returned home safely from his camping holiday. He had a great time with lovely weather, but was thoroughly fed-up with camping food. Sophie was fine, as her mum had taken a family sized pack of instant mash, so she was happy.

August 12th

Had an email from my ex-husband to say he was stopping my maintenance for Ashley from September. Great, just what I need, good job I had put the money aside for the Robbie tickets. He has always been on and off with payments and has this strange idea that he can dictate how this money is dished out. Perhaps if he had to keep a teenage boy for more than a couple of weeks in the summer, he would realize I wasn't squandering it on booze and fags. I thought after all these years we had moved on and stopped playing games, and hurting each other. For goodness sake, there are only another six months to go and then that would be it, we can look back and be proud. We had made it - brought up the kids, been polite to each other and shown the kids how mature we are.

137

It was so sad that marriage number two had not worked out, it had all started off with such promise. I was just recovering from marriage number one, which came to a very brief and untimely end when I was invited to a friend's wedding reception. I went along with another girlfriend and half way through the night, feeling a little morose and sorry for myself, decided I had had enough, so my friend and I went for a walk along the banks of the River Thames in Windsor. As we were walking and talking I declared that the next man I met would own a boat and what's more we would marry and have our wedding reception at Sir Christopher Wren's old house on the Windsor and Eton bridge and live happily ever after. Some of this was to come true.

So after marriage number one broke down I had found a place to rent on the other side of the town. I could still cycle to work and afford to pay the rent, it meant I could leave our marital home prior to it being sold, as I really did not want to live alone and my first husband preferred not to see me. It was all very sad and raw.

After answering an advert in the local paper, I went to view a shared maisonette where I would have my own bedroom. It was perfect and the landlord was charming, we hit it off immediately and I arranged to move in. He even said he could borrow a van from work and help me move my stuff, so I was over the moon. I told my Mum all about it and she seemed pleased for me, it meant I could keep my job and I wouldn't be living on my own.

"He said I could move in straight away," I excitedly told my Mum.

"I bet he did - Karen do you know what you are doing?" she asked worriedly.

He kept his word and helped me move. He then had to go out, but would be back at nine thirty, and asked if I would like to nip to the local pub for last orders. In the pub we started talking and I asked him about himself and what his hobbies were. He told me he had a boat moored at Old Windsor that he was renovating and would take me out on it some time.

I nearly fell off my chair, I knew there and then that the man sitting in front of me was destined to be husband number two, I could hardly wait to get to work on Monday morning and tell my friend all about it. She would never believe me, who would think that fate would work that fast?

August 13th

Sam is in a bad mood after ruining another of my throws. I have therefore taken away his bone. Not sure if this will work, but at least I feel better.

Asked James to show me how to listen to voice mail messages on my phone this morning, as apparently Sarah has left me loads and as I had not answered she thought I was ignoring her. Terry got a bit annoyed - I think he's a bit jealous of James' technical abilities.

Had an e-mail from someone by mistake, this is the first time this has happened to me. It was the strangest e-mail from a man who had contacted us previously about going to see him in April to quote for some work. He had explained he lived in the next village and sounded really friendly and I said we would look forward to meeting him and his wife, but we never heard back from him. Anyway the gist of this mistaken email was that he had been to his house in April and, after cleaning out the barn, had started a bonfire and as everything was a bit damp, he thought a bit of petrol would help it on its way. He managed to set fire to himself; his jeans caught alight and he couldn't put them out and was engulfed within seconds. His wife phoned the Pompiers who summoned the helicopter and he was rushed to Rennes Hospital by air ambulance. Once there he was admitted into the burns ward, then transferred to Lyon for more specialist treatment to his burns. He was then transferred again, three months later to England.

It was when I read the next bit I nearly fell off my chair, I was mortified to read the exploits of this stranger, 'I am making a good recovery and hope one day to be able to walk again.' No wonder he never got in touch about the work on his house. Although he had sent it by mistake (he e-mailed me to let me know this), I emailed him with my sympathies - you can't just ignore an email like that can you, even if it was sent by error?

I told Terry about it and he said it reminded him of the time he was in Ireland with his mates helping them to put a roof on their house. They were having a bonfire in the back garden when someone unknown to Terry threw petrol on it. He had been standing very close to the fire and when it flared up he managed to jump backwards, but not without damage. It was only when he got home that he realised his left eyebrow and half of his moustache were missing, but as he said, it could have been so much worse.

This unexpected e-mailers' story only goes to show you how dangerous it is. Terry warned me, "You must be careful with your bonfires, I know how you love them, but just take it easy." It's nice to know how much he cares.

August 15th

Phoned Sarah, she is fine and working hard, so that when she goes back to Uni she will have some money in the bank, which means that she can do less paid work and concentrate on her education. I suggested that she cancel her Sky subscription, at least that way there would be less choice of telly to watch during the day. She has an audition next week for Deal or no Deal; they had phoned her and she was looking forward to winning and paying off all her student debts. She told me she would also take me on holiday. Well, we will have to wait and see - I am still waiting for my Mothers' Day present. She has given up smoking, her dad has promised her £350 if she manages to do so.

Mum phoned and was feeling rather stressed about the upcoming inquest into Joy's death. She feels she needs to go and was hoping some questions might be answered, but was not looking forward to it. She asked me if I thought Sarah would like to go as she is studying Psychology.

Gran was fine, although a little confused still thinking Grandad is sleeping in her bed and that the 'other woman' is keeping him very busy, as she can hear them 'having a jump' in the room above her. One of the residents, a man, had been weeing in the corridor outside her room and sometimes got confused and entered Gran's room. She was not at all happy about this and told Mum that she always told him to 'bugger off', 'out of it' and 'be on yer way'. She had enjoyed her egg custard and polished off two glasses of sherry, so Mum had left her happy and contented. Mum told me that she had been glad to get out of the house saying, "I am just about to divorce your bloody dad. He is driving me mad. He only went out in the garden in his slippers this morning, came in and walked cat mess all up the stairs and around the bedroom before I caught him, I could kill him," she moaned.

She explained that they were having problems with the neighbour's cats doing their business in the garden.

"You need to borrow Sam," I suggested.

"I don't think you are allowed to murder your neighbour's pets in England," she laughed.

I explained that I thought he would just frighten them and then they wouldn't have a problem, and if he did kill any of them it would be survival of the fittest - you know, natural selection and all that. Still angry and annoyed at my Dad and his cat shit slippers she was off on one.

"You can't do that, its murder; you'd have the RSPCA after you, you'll be all for euthanasia next," she cried. Well you have got a point there Mum, I secretly thought.

I haven't always been a doggy person. After waving our first dog off on the bus with my Dad to the vets, and Dad coming back without him, when I was three years old, I never thought I would have one in my life again. The dog had bit me on the lip and my Mum found the dog and I covered in blood. Needless to say, I had always given dogs a wide berth since, preferring to share my company with cats. Sam had been the first dog to infiltrate this and I was now swaying in the doggy direction; cats seemed no fun at all. They were too independent and suspicious, whereas dogs are so loveable and don't get moody with you for going out and leaving them on their own. They are simply glad you are back; they just want to love you, be your friend and follow you everywhere and you sure as hell know when you have stepped in dog shit before entering the house.

August 20th

So boring; Ashley is still in bed, Terry is at work and the dog is on a final warning after eating my sunglasses and chewing my best handbag. There is only one thing for it, I will have to do the shopping. At this time of the year everywhere is busy and you have to fight with the tourists for a parking place, then try not to ram them with your shopping trolley, as they saunter around the shop looking at all the products, as if they had never seen food for sale before. It drives me crazy, so at this time of the year, I prefer not to go shopping, but as we had run out of wine, I really had no choice.

I once had a friend back in England who taught me to go round the Supermarket the wrong way, so that you can fit all your alcohol into your trolley. Obviously this only applies if you are having a party or if you have a serious drink problem - my friend had the latter.

Sometimes it would play havoc with his job as a postman. He had no problem getting up as he was always shit faced by nine o'clock in the evening and fast asleep. No, he had a problem with finding a loo on his postal round, sometimes having to do 'number twos' in the garden of an unsuspecting member of the public. Luckily there was always enough junk mail to wipe his bum. I missed him, his girlfriend and their madness.

Over the years we have been privy to his experimental distillation of alcohol, which unfortunately ended up with it catching fire. His creative lamp shade, he made out of old coloured lighters - this was certainly a roaring success and looked stunning until he changed the light bulb for a higher wattage. It had immediately exploded and burst into flames.

Then there was the amazing Christmas dinner that he cooked for us all. After some gentle dancing in the lounge, we were prohibited from being too energetic, as his downstairs elderly neighbour Maud, had an ornate ceiling. Sadly the dinner was ruined. The large pile of driftwood that he had collected was propped up precariously by the cooker and had caught fire. We therefore had to abandon our Christmas feast and retire to the pub. The fire was safely put out by my husband, with the use of the water from a nearby goldfish tank. Terry later said, "I don't know why I killed the fish, I just panicked when I saw the flames."

Our friend's girlfriend wasn't happy though, and referred to Terry as 'the goldfish murderer' for many years. I suppose with all these fire related incidents it came as no surprise when their flat and the rest of the house burnt down one day. However, surprisingly on this occasion it was not his fault, he had become a victim of an arson attack.

After completing his postal round, popping in his local for a few beers and picking up the shopping, he had gone home for a lie down. Soundly asleep the phone rang and rang and rang, eventually waking him up. It was his girlfriend; she was on her way home on the bus after attending her father's funeral and, understandably, was a bit down. She fancied a drink and some company, so he agreed to meet her in the pub, pulled on his jacket, got his bike down the stairs and went to meet her.

She had arrived before him and was sitting at the bar drinking her Vodka, with a pint of Guinness chaser, when suddenly a neighbour burst in screaming that the postie's house was on fire. He explained he had just come by the building, and that there were flames billowing out of the upstairs windows, and the firemen from two fire engines were beating back the flames. Maud had got out and also the lad in the flat opposite them, but there was no sign of her boyfriend. Tears started to roll down her face as she ran from the bar to see for herself, surely she could not bury her father and lose the love of her life on the same day? As she sped down the street and along dog shit alley, there were people everywhere, but still no sign of her beloved, just billowing flames, fire fighters and noise. Then out of the smoke appeared a man, riding a sit-up-and-beg bike with cow horns, it was him, he had got out.

He explained that, before going to the pub, he had decided to call into the florist to buy her a bunch of daffodils to cheer her up, but when he arrived the barman had explained what had happened, that she had heard the news and run off leaving her bags and drinks behind. Gulping down the Vodka and Guinness he mounted his mighty stead and hurtled after her.

It turned out that the house had been attacked deliberately. The ground floor flat had been empty and a fire had been started with petrol on the old mattresses and rubbish inside, from there it spread quickly engulfing the rest of the property just shortly after he had left.

It was a nasty business, the guy who had lived in the top flat had recently been accused of being a paedophile by the young brain damaged lad who had lived with him for years. He had eventually plucked up the courage to report the abuse and the goings on of this animal. The man had been arrested and the young lad taken away to safety.

He told us about this in his annual Christmas phone-call last year, stating that they had managed to get a nearby flat on the same terrace, on the same floor, with the same lay-out. Fortunately, the new flat had a much better view of the harbour. I asked him if they had managed to save anything, especially his vast music collection. Terry was more concerned about his extensive porn collection, and Star Trek DVDs.

"No we lost just about everything, all gone. If it hadn't gone up in smoke, then it was too badly damaged to keep," he explained.

"What a shame," my husband said, sadly shaking his head, "all those films, he took ages to make them."

He had with the aid of a remote control and two video recorders, compiled his own adult sex movies, cutting out all the rubbishy bits and getting it down to twenty minutes of pure filth or, as he put it, the only bit worth watching. He even had an idea of marketing his newly arranged adult films with the logo 'Five minute fumbles, for people who lead busy lives.' After all, he explained, "The people who buy this kind of material don't buy it to watch the story line or listen to the awful music. They don't want any of that lead-in stuff - all soft focus and simmering intentions, no, you want to get straight in there with the proper stuff."

I didn't like to ask his girlfriend, but this gave me a sneaky suspicion that he probably was rubbish at foreplay. He did have a point though. All those adult movie-makers could save a fortune by only creating half a film. After the main event in the middle, it could just be a blank tape as who honestly watches the whole film? I think he was on to a winner, no one could care less if Heidi and Claus ran off into the sunset whilst being chased by her bisexual husband, Mannfrid and his two nubile, very well endowed cleaners, Lottie and Lola. And let's face it what saddo would complain about missing the end of a film like that? No one would take you seriously if you asked for your money back.

August 21st

Finally booked a holiday, we are off to Rhodes again. It will be the same as last year, except we are going for two weeks this time.

Two whole weeks with someone to talk to every day! A most welcome break from, 'she who shall not be named'. No mad customers phoning me demanding we quote for work the following day, as they are only here for a three day visit, and forgot to book an appointment before they arrived. Or waking us up at nine o'clock, on a Sunday morning, to discuss their damp proof course. It will be bliss - just the two of us. We always have wonderful holidays together with magical things happening. Oh, and lots of books to read whilst lying on a sunbed looking out to sea - what could be better?

We should also be able to go and see Sarah, which will be fantastic as she has just moved into a new flat and I am dying to visit her and her boyfriend.

Phoned my Mum and asked if she and Dad would like to house and dog sit. My Dad loves our dog but Mum won't let him have one of his own. She is still a cat person at heart, despite next doors wayward moggies. He once said he envied me, all he ever wanted in life was a dog and some chickens. It is a shame we can't have chickens any more, but the dog would kill them. Mind you, when we did kill one of ours to eat, my Dad went mad and said we would be eating the children next.

Note: start making a list for my Dad of jobs to do whilst we are away. This will keep him out of Mum's way and stop him having bonfires in the driveway, or using Terry's best wood to make bird tables.

August 23rd

I have given up smoking - thought I would support Sarah. Ashley has agreed to give up in September for Sophie, so I really should set a good example. Sarah had been to see her doctor and got some tablets to help her, but I will go cold turkey. Terry said he didn't know why I was bothering, my ex husband wouldn't give me £350 for giving up. At least I knew where their maintenance money was going.

Emailed Annie to let her know we would be coming to England. As we were flying to Rhodes from Gatwick, we would be staying over and would love to see her if that was okay. She thought that Paul would be back from Afghanistan by then and we would be able to see him. She was counting the days and was really looking forward to his return. If he didn't hurry up home she would end up attending AA. Mr Patel in the local off-license had become a personal friend and she had the Indian takeaway on speed dial. She had given up internet dating after a few encounters. She said she was getting too fussy and they always disappointed. It is a shame she never made a career as a high-class hooker, she would have been so good at it - all that sex and getting paid for it, she could have even put her sexy underwear on expenses.

Unlike me she didn't have off-days and was always up for it. I don't know how she did it or why. Personally I think you can't beat a nice cup of cocoa, a good book and an early night. Sometimes husbands are over-rated, but then I had had three.

August 25th

Had a phone call from someone wanting a quote for a new roof. The only problem was that he did not have the full address of the property or know exactly where it was. I told him it was not a problem and asked if he had a photo he could e-mail to me. He didn't, but he apparently knew it's rough location, when he told me where it was I had to bite my lip to stop myself coming out with 'Oh, you mean dodge city.' You really are stuffed buying a house there, those cowboys can smell fresh meat from a mile off and Friday nights are like something from the OK Corral. You are surrounded by builders, plumbers, painters and gardeners before you can unpack and steady the horses.

All he wanted was a ballpark figure to re-tile one hundred and twenty-five square meters, as they were on the verge of purchasing the property and were costing out any refurbishments they may need to make in the future. The roof was watertight and it would appear there were no problems with it. This was purely an exercise to find out the cost of worst scenarios. Had a word with Terry and after his disbelief that anyone could possibly want a price for a roof without him looking at it, he worked out a rough estimate. You do get all sorts.

"Sounds like some more poor souls are destined to a future of a half finished home and poverty and with their enquiry about the roof, their estate agent should be renamed 'I saw you coming,'" he laughed, before heading off to his cinema.

Talking of which, the woman who enquired about renting my friend's house at Christmas has not got back to me. After asking me to hold the property for her, she emailed me a list of questions:

Does it have heating apart from the wood burner?

Will there be plenty of places to go out to on New Year's Eve?

I had responded, but perhaps not with the answers she was hoping for, stating that it was an old farmhouse and it did not have central heating, so therefore she might like to bring her slippers and pyjamas (and any other warm clothes they had). I added that the French (around here) spend New Year's Eve with their families and therefore nothing much is open at that time, or any other time come to think about it. I hope I did not put her off, but it is strange that she has not got back to me. Perhaps they preferred somewhere warmer and livelier? I don't blame them - I do!

August 30th

Back to school tomorrow for Ashley and it will be his last year. I can hardly believe it has gone so quickly. He has worked so hard, but has often been penalised for being English and had to suffer racial abuse from some pupils and staff.

My brother phoned me last July to tell me that his son had got twenty out of twenty in his English test but they had marked him down three points because he is English, to which my nephew kindly pointed out, that in fact he held a Dutch passport. This happens a lot, either that or arguing about the pronunciation of Mickey Mouse with your English teacher, who always instinctively seems to hate the English kids in her class, possibly afraid they will make a show of them.

In all the years we have been here the only teachers I have had to go into school to see are the English teachers. It follows a pattern where either Ashley is saying too much and correcting her or he won't speak and refuses to help. He and an American boy had a game going for a while to see how long they could go without speaking in a lesson. You would think that English teachers would be happy to embrace all things English and find it a bonus to have a native speaker in the class. It may have something to do with the French thinking they know it all, but in our experience it has been hard work, they eye you with suspicion and then it is an uphill battle to win their trust and actually get a decent result in the class.

Don't get me wrong I love the French and I love all things French. It really is the most beautiful country with miles of wonderful open roads, amazing cuisine and fantastic beaches, mountains and skiing - truly a gem in our world. It has everything all in one country and is really magnificent. Just don't think you can move here and be French, you will always be an outsider - never quite getting the joke, not have mammy's secret recipe for Poulet au Pot, never knowing when to kiss two times or three, say bonjour or bonsoir. Little things like that set us apart and we will always be étrangers.

Anyway, Ashley is back to the Lycée tomorrow. Let's hope he can keep his nose clean for one more year and leave on a happy note. I do not relish the prospect of being called in to see his headmistress - I'm not sure if it is her, or the picture of the Pope behind her desk, which scares me the most.

Loonies Lovers and Letters

September 1st

The day of the inquest into Joy's death. Mum and Auntie Jayne were attending. It is to be held in St John's Wood Coroners' Court in London, so they had set off once again on the train, with their packed lunches and thermos flasks. Mum, in her usual organized fashion, had booked the train tickets well in advance, making sure they got the best deal. They were not looking forward to it, but hoped to glean more information concerning Joy's life and what had happened to her. Auntie Jayne was hoping it would all be done and dusted before lunch, as she had an appointment for some Botox treatment in Brent Cross.

We were still finding it impossible to understand what had been going on in Joy's head and why she had just given up, it was all so dreadful. It would seem that if you didn't have a partner, you could just slip through the net, nobody would notice you had gone and you could die alone, without anyone being aware of the fact. I think this is the bit that hurt my Mum the most. To know that she had been such a wanted child, to have remained loved so much and cared for, yet it all ended in a completely opposite way.

Mum had arranged for Joy's body to be brought back home to Leicester and cremated. Her ashes were to be interned on her parents' grave, My Mum felt she had done the right thing. She had found an old notebook in which Joy and had made summaries and scribbled thoughts, with questions like 'Who will deal with all this mess when I am dead?' These transcripts about death and dying had deeply shocked my Mum and Dad.

"Nobody writes like that if they are sane," my Dad had sadly commented. He just didn't understand how anyone could reach such a drastic state of mind. I too had read the notes and was not as shocked as Mum and Dad.

Many years ago, I had been in a similar dark place emotionally and had jottings and poems in my notepad that confirmed this. I had been on my own with two small children and living miles away from my family and friends, trying to cope with running a holiday complex and bar. The kids were all over the place. Sarah blamed me and vented her anger at anyone and everyone. Ashley couldn't keep a dry pair of pants on at school.

I felt a failure, it wasn't what I wanted or expected and for a little while I seriously thought that I would be better off dead. I had written it all down and, looking back now, I can still feel that agony of loss. I wrote a few poems and they did help, it's true that getting it down on paper does seem to ease the pain. However, it takes a long time to mend.

After splitting up with my first husband, I had married my landlord. We had the reception at Wren's Old House Hotel, as I had predicted. We spent many happy years on that boat each summer and had three wonderful children together. Sadly though it didn't last and the romance that was so full of possibilities faded. We had our fair share of ups and downs and when Matthew died we both quite literally fell to pieces, neither of us could cope and it was impossible to mend ourselves, let alone our relationship.

We did try, we tried really hard - even going on to have Ashley, but the damage had been done and we would not be able to support each other again. There was a cloud of resentment that only bereavement can bring to a marriage, neither of us wanting to take the other down by talking about our loss. We would therefore bottle it up and ultimately talk to someone else about it instead of each other - it was easier that way. We were lost souls floundering around in the dark, each begging someone, anyone, to help us. We weren't equipped to understand each other and so we lost our love and little by little the promises we had made to each other disappeared.

Luckily for me when we moved to North Devon my ex-husband had sacked the old caretaker, and had employed a new one. The new caretaker kept me sane; he would turn up for work and I would be in tears over one thing or other. On one occasion my ex had sent me a bouquet as this had appeased me in the past, and I was on the floor crying at how he thought he could win me back with a bunch of carnations - I hated carnations.

"He didn't even know me," I sobbed really feeling sorry for myself. The caretaker would put the kettle on and I would carry on howling and wailing at the awfulness of my life and how unfairly I had been treated. He didn't say a word, just nodded and made more tea. He was my rock, my salvation - he became my best friend and eventually my third husband. He saved me just by being there when I needed someone and had no one to whine to. If only Joy had found a Terry - everyone needs one.

September 3rd

The man my husband is currently working for is steadily becoming known as 'he who shall not be told'. We had a customer a few years ago we knew as 'she who shall not be named'. We called her this as we spent so much time talking about her and this guy is fast becoming even worse and that is saying something.

Things have not improved on site, in fact it has got worse as no one is now talking to Terry, apart from James his labourer, and as we pay him he doesn't really have a choice. With Terry being a sociable guy, it is getting him down - that and the fact that the customer is hopeless and cannot take direction. We now have to have a steward's inquiry every teatime. We are still no nearer to finding out what this man is on. Seriously, it comes to something when you can't even pass a civil word to your builder. I really feel like going over there and giving him a piece of my mind, but Terry has told me not to. He reminded me that if I want some spending money for our holiday then getting sacked is not a good move.

This holiday cannot come fast enough, I just hope Terry doesn't hit 'he who shall not be told' before we go. He has been so preoccupied with the problem that all he wants to do when he comes home is slip into his cinema and escape. "If only life was like Star Trek," he told me, "we could live in peace by following the prime directive." I could do with getting my husband back and adding a little romance into our relationship, not that it has ever had much before - I mean who has their first kiss in dog shit alley?

We lived in North Devon at the time and dog shit alley was a well known short cut. It earned this title because it was unfortunately shielded from the road and all the dog owners could get away with letting their dogs foul down there. Mind you, on reflection, they did it all over the town. I remembered that when I had first visited the area years ago with my parents I had vowed to never come back again, declaring it was full of hills and dog mess. It certainly hadn't changed much.

On the night of our first kiss, we were stumbling home giggly and slightly drunk - finally falling into an embrace, and managing to not get covered in dog shit. After months of friendship it felt right - we were mates out having a good time together, but as we got home and started to sober up we both had cold feet about taking things any further. Terry suggested we put the kettle on and have a nice cup of tea.

I knew then that I had found my Mr Right, he was one of the good guys. A pleasant, thoughtful, entertaining, gorgeous man, with common decency who knew how to treat a lady well. He had good old fashioned manners and was someone who didn't just jump on women - he was the perfect boyfriend. He did have a lousy dress sense, needed a decent haircut and was obsessed by motor bikes and Star Trek, but hey, no one's perfect.

Many years later I found out it was not just me who had been petrified of moving on to the next stage. He had been celibate for two years and wasn't totally sure he wanted a girlfriend. He had been hurt badly and thought women were trouble, so we were both taking a big risk.

September 5th

Things to do:

Repair loo seat

Find out why there are 'holes' in the dog food cupboard

Post bills (do internet banking first)

Find my slippers

Service the lawn mover and replace the belt

I was running around like a mad woman, trying to get beds made up and clean everywhere. This was not helped by the fact that Terry decided to rub down the walls in the bedroom above the dining room, which we have been renovating, and the dust went all over the house. Anyway, we will have to sleep in there when my Mum and Dad arrive so it is a complete mad house with quilts and pillowcases everywhere. To make matters more difficult is the fact that my parents have to sleep in separate rooms as my Dad snores and Mum has hot flushes.

Sam thinks it is tremendous fun and when my back is turned he runs off with the pillowcases - so far I have lost two. Terry said he does not know why I bother and that my Mum always does a lovely job with the cleaning whenever she visits, so I might as well sit down and forget about it. Forget about it? My Mum is a fully paid up, bona-fide member of the clean and tidy perfect housewife brigade. I don't know how she does it, but beds are always made in her house, there is never any fluff on the loo, dust on her pictures or cobwebs - come to think of it, I don't think I have ever seen any dirt in her house at all (well not since my brother and I left home). She also manages somehow to bake her own biscuits, pickle beetroot, make chutney and jam, cook and decorate her own Christmas cake by July. Not only that, she still manages to get her hair done and shave her legs, and is the member of several committees in the village.

But men just don't get it. If Terry had his way we would live in a house with a motorbike as a feature in the lounge and a poster of the star ship enterprise on the wall. When we first moved here, not knowing the system, I had arranged an approximate date for our furniture (which was in storage) to arrive in France. With a country that invented laissez-fare, I figured that the date for our move was not set in stone. How wrong could I have been? When buying and selling houses in France you could set your watch by the accuracy of the Notaire, they keep to their dates and nothing can change it, even the small problem of having no furniture. So with no hope of a reprieve, the removal company could only deliver on the date I had given them and we could only move on the date the Notaire had given us, three months earlier. Luckily in those days we were young, carefree and very stupid. The furniture would arrive two weeks after we had moved in, but with a fearless excitement we were not put off.

After we had signed the contracts and been given the keys for our new house, we asked the previous owner, Gilles, if he would mind taking us to the house as, despite driving around for two days after we had agreed to buy it and forwarding vast amounts of money for deposits and final payment, we still didn't have a bloody clue where the house was - absolutely no idea. We had spent a few fretful nights back in England wondering what on earth we had done I can tell you. Anyway Gilles had a good laugh and kindly presented us to our new home.

With no furniture we just had to make the best of it. It was like Scrap Heap Challenge and luckily for us Gilles had not thrown everything away. We managed to find an old table, a coat stand, chest of drawers and a mattress, where we would all end up sleeping together. Therefore, in theory Terry has slept with most of my family. The greatest thing we discovered was an old car seat! Having no comfortable chairs, we took it in turns as to who could sit in it, we all loved it and it was a very sad day many years later when it was relegated to the dump.

So back to the cleaning, Terry immediately shot off to his cinema and, taking a bottle of wine with him, didn't look back. He was not going to help me with the mammoth task of housework and tidying up. This is guaranteed to make me angry and to play the martyr, 'Oh no, don't worry about me', 'I will only be up until midnight cleaning'. Terry knew me only too well and was keeping out of the way.

It is only my Mum and Dad, but I just want everything to be perfect for them. I could not bear her telling my brother I had turned into a lazy so-and-so, even if the first thing she would do would be to rearrange my pantry. Mind you, I don't know why I get so worked up - it is crazy. We had once fallen out and didn't speak for a long time, all because I left my brother at the village fete and he had to walk home, I thought he was on a promise with the young French girl he was dancing all night with.

He was drunk and had got lost, finally turning up at six in the morning complete with a detour past the Zoo. Mum said I should have looked after him and it was all my fault. I told her and Dad to mind their own business, which resulted in a monumental row. Things were a little strained for a while after. I wouldn't mind, but my brother was forty at the time.

Still I guess in the eyes of your parents you never grow up and I will always be the older sister who should have looked out for her little brother. We finally forgot the row, as life is too short and we realised that you only get one set of parents (if you are lucky) and that mine would do anything for me and my brother - even fighting our battles. I had been blessed with the most thoughtful parents in the world and, as Terry kept reminding me, I am very loved. I am also very short tempered and stubborn, which was how we got in the mess in the first place.

September 6th

We don't just have mad customers, many of our customers over the years have become very good friends. In fact that is where we get the majority of our work, it comes from recommendations or just old customers wanting more work done. We have therefore never had to advertise since running a business in France, relying on a free listing on the ARSE (Anglo Rural Society for Ex-Pats) website and word of mouth.

We have been lucky to survive without having to travel far and wide and to be able to choose who we work for. Although, Alana was struck off the list a few years ago, the final straw came when she put Terry's bright yellow metal spirit level on her fire and tried to burn it thinking it was wood. She had also tried to pay him with a hat stand instead of cash on one occasion, saying that I had admired it. This was the final straw and he declared that he just could not cope with the madness - well when he was trying to work and could not join in, it was not funny.

This has not made us rich and relying on this kind of approach is not for the faint hearted, especially when your husband is fond of spending the central heating oil money on booze. We have, however, made some good friends and, over the years, have laughed with them and even cried with them, usually about the price the electrician wants to charge. One of them had e-mailed me that morning to say they will be over this weekend and would we like to have dinner with them on Saturday night? Oh, and did I want a sliced loaf from Tesco?

The phone had rung that morning with an inquiry, "I saw your advertisement on the Anglo ex-pats site," a charming and rather posh sounding lady said, "we have just moved to a beautiful old chateau, don't you know, it's practically Versailles. It is in the next village, you might know it - the manor house near the church – we are practically neighbours. Anyway, I digress", she carried on before I could get a word in, "we saw your advertisement and would like a quote for a complete renovation - you know the bloody works my dear." She reeled off the list, "Replacing all the windows with bespoke handmade ones, a new central heating system, re-wire, sandblasting old fireplaces, all the doors and kitchen to be hand-made and fitted, installing an AGA, under floor heating and building a swimming pool. That's about the size of it – is that something hubby could do?"

Before I could answer she was off again.

"We have tremendous plans!" she gasped, at last sounding out of breath, and obviously very excited. I said we would be more than happy to visit and provide a quote.

"We have sold our house in London for a ridiculous price, do you know Notting Hill? You wouldn't believe how much we got for it! A little town house, and for the same price we have a manor now," she enthused eagerly, "so we have cash, don't you know, for the renovation work. My husband, Lucien, is retired, was big in the city, before it went tits up, don't you know, so we are in a spiffing situation, should be top notch," she carried on, offering the carrot of what sounded like years worth of work, "I just need to find a little part-time job, you know in a florists or the like, that would be ideal. Just to bring in a little petty cash for treats, don't you know, and what with no school fees to pay, well we should be tip top!" She added optimistically.

I arranged for Terry to visit to get some quotes together and gave her the name of the electrician and plumber we use.

"The children have started at the local primary school. Tarquin, Edward, and Cosima just love it, dear. How long did it take for your sprogs to become fluent?" She enquired and added, amused, "you don't happen to know anyone who could give us lessons to teach the lingo darling, preferably not a native, as if they are French we won't have a bloody clue!" she laughed, enjoying her own witticism. She was starting to get on my nerves now, and my coffee was getting cold. As I tried to round up the conversation, sadly she hadn't finished yet.

"Oh, and do you have a contact for an English speaking Doctor? My poor Lucien's hernia is giving him dreadful jip."

"Doctor Le Boucher is very good, speaks English too," I informed her.

"The butcher! The doctor is called the butcher, ah, very amusing!"

He is very amusing, the last time I had seen him he was paddling in my friend's river in his very brief underpants on a hot August day. I asked if she had health insurance as you have to pay

"What, it's not free?" she asked surprised, "I thought France was a republic."

"Well, sometimes you can't beat the good old NHS." I said.

I reminded her about ARSE, where you can find everything and anything and get information from people who know what they are talking about, oh, and quite a lot who know nothing at all, but love to make it up.

You see that's the point, you arrive with good intentions to learn the language, even enrolling in classes. You try to converse with everyone you meet and after two years, when you can just about get by, you give up. You have the basics for a conversation, you can make an appointment at the doctors and a reservation at the local restaurant, fill out your tax return and buy your shopping. With the aid of ARSE you can find English speaking builders, hairdressers, chiropodists, plumbers, doctors, dentists, tree surgeons, architects and someone else to fill out your tax return.

You have learned the essentials, become fully integrated with the ex-pat lifestyle and their contacts and, let's face it, who wants to watch French telly when you can have Sky installed for the price of your TV license. This means you can have it all, English TV, radio, and to my husband's delight, Russia today and Al Jazeera. Who needs to know what the French are up to? You can almost forget you are in France, apart from not being able to get a decent loaf of bread and the shops shutting for two hours at lunch time.

I had a sneaky suspicion though that I would be hearing from Mrs Lahr de dah in a few months time explaining that she and her husband had scaled down on their renovation project because, 'You would not believe what the electrician wanted to charge!' and that she had failed to get a job and was now taking in washing.

I know it sounds cruel, but I can't tell you the amount of times I have seen this. They start off with wanting handmade bespoke windows, under floor heating and a swimming pool then, a couple of years down the line when they have spent all their money, they have Brico Depot UPVC windows, a wood burning stove and a plastic paddling pool in the front garden.

Anyway, our good friends, and customers, were coming over at the weekend to inspect the UPVC windows Terry had fitted. I should not be as rude about the ex-pats website, as it is a mine of information. You really can find out everything you need to know about Normandy, on a typical day you will see:

FOR SALE - Budgerigar and cage - one careful owner

WANTED – Bantam cockerels

WANTED - Well-endowed Billy goat needed for my lonely Nanny (photo required)

English speaking accountant needed to fill in tax return

Where to buy suet?

WANTED – Brave child to ride enthusiastic pony

Hammond organ for sale VGC

Why are electricians so expensive?

Lesbian gay bars near Domfront

Riding boots for sale - 25 euros, good condition (only worn once)

English   speaking
DENTIST/DOCTOR/VET/HAIRDRESSER/GARDENER

How to get cheap phone calls to the UK?

Horse muck free to collector

And so on...I sometimes wonder how we would have survived without it.

September 12th

Mum and Dad arrived safely. Mum had driven her car over and it resembled Santa's sleigh as it was packed to the gunnels with goodies. It is just as well she had not been stopped by Customs at Portsmouth for one of their spot searches, as she would still be there now trying to repack it. Consequently, it took ages to unpack all the surprises she had bought for us and all the luxuries she had for my brother. She was going down to stay with him in Brittany for a week before we go away. Frederic had vacated the caravan and moved in with Ludo, although he told Sid he had left his weight training gear behind in case my Dad fancied pumping some iron.

It looked like Mum had cleared the shelves at Asda with all the baked beans and veggie burger packets she had for my brother. It would sure be windy down in Sion les Mînes for some time and he still only had an outside loo. My poor mum. It is lovely to see them and wonderful to have company, even if they follow me around everywhere. Between my Dad and the dog it was a competition to see who could walk to heel the best, or trip me up.

Alana popped in, so that was a nice treat for my mum, she's a bit like Sarah and loves to witness a true crazy woman at large. She and Les had been going home, but suddenly realised that they had forgotten to buy any wine so had delayed their departure to go shopping. She said she was not sure if they would be back again this year, as it gets too cold in their house in the Autumn and Winter, but wished my mum a happy Christmas and said she would see them next year. In the meantime, as they were staying an extra day did I fancy a quick trip to Rennes, as she had to pick up some bits she was storing at a friend's Brocante. I said I would love to. I don't get much excitement and I agreed to meet her after lunch.

This proved to be a bad move, and although she had abstained from her usual liquid lunch, she was still quite strange. We set off and alarm bells should have rung when she filled her diesel car with petrol and we had to make an emergency pit stop at the local garage to have the petrol drained and cleaned out. Two hours later we were on our way. There wasn't a lot of traffic and, having got to Rennes in record time, we then proceeded to spend the next three hours lost in the city. She had left her friend's address and phone number at home and couldn't quite remember how to get there. This necessitated a lot of stopping and starting to ask for directions. We eventually visited the local police station, I thought they were going to arrest her, just to shut her up.

Bouncing through the double doors into the reception we must have looked quite a sight. As Alana, was wearing a tie dye t-shirt that barely covered her midriff and her unrestrained breasts were swinging wildly, as she sashayed in with her finest showing off French, complete with hand gestures, she had caught the dozing Gendarmes eyes. As she had travelled extensively through France as a teenager and learned the language, she took control. I'm not sure what was happening with her accent or translation, as no one seemed to understand what the hell she was saying. Their eyes were glued to the hypnotic swinging of her downwardly pointing erect nipples. She was under the impression that the coppers fancied her and were flirting with her - and so she had joined in, toying outrageously with the poor desk sergeant. It was quite terrifying.

"Well they were a bunch of strapping boys." She smiled as we finally left.

I truly thought she was going to ask one of them for their phone number, she was totally unaware that they were sniggering behind her back. No wonder they think us English women are always up for it, Alana had put the women's liberation back a decade by trying to use her womanly charms, I just shook my head.

"Come on Madame Bovary let's get you in the car before you can do anymore damage, you little tease." I joked with her.

We finally, more through luck than judgment, found her friends shop. I asked if I could borrow her friend's phone as it was now quite late and we wouldn't make it home before dark.

"Oh you can use this thing if you know how," Alana said, on hearing this request, and offered me her mobile phone.

"I didn't know you had this? We could have called your friend on it," I said, exasperated with her by now.

"Yes we could have, but you shouldn't use your phone whilst driving"

"Yeah I've heard that one too Alana," I said, making a mental note to decline any invitation for an afternoon out the next time she asked me. I blame care in the community, I thought to myself. We got home six hours later in one piece and I was relieved to be home and safe. I said I would keep an eye on her house when I walked the dog down the lane and let her know if anything needed to be done. She thanked me and, in a cloud of black smoke, shot off up the drive taking most of our gravel with her, again preferring to drive on the banking for some reason. At least I would be able to gather my holly and mistletoe in peace without her screaming abuse at me this year. It was a nice feeling knowing she wouldn't be back until the Spring.

One year when she was over she told me off for going in the fields near her house to gather holly, saying that it was private land. I told her to piss off - she was clearly starting her festive celebrations early, as I could smell the booze from a field away. She later when sober, apologised and said she thought I was a hunter! More likely she didn't want anyone down there witnessing her alcoholic stupors. Later that night to relax, I read my e-mails there was one from Sarah telling me that Robbie and Gary Barlow's first single is out so I Googled it and watched it on YouTube. I couldn't believe what I was seeing - was it a Mickey take of Broke Back Mountain or were they going for the pink pound, I just didn't get it, it was so overtly camp. I shouted Ashley and he had a good laugh, "I told you Mum, he's a screaming homo. "

"But he just got married," I stressed

"Elton John, Mum, that's all I'm saying, Elton John," sniggered Ashley, as he went back to his bedroom.

He did have a point.

I don't think I want to go and see them, though, so I will tell Sarah to forget about buying any tickets. I had really gone off Robbie, what with him getting married and now this gay side. I think I might have to look for someone a bit more butch and I certainly won't bother buying his new CD in England.

September 21st

Left for England, taking James, our labourer, with us. This was good as I needed some help with my mobile. Once again, I couldn't work out how to find out how much credit I had, or turn it off so that it would not ring when we were on the plane to Greece.

Terry, in a resigned tone, said,

"You have waited all this time, didn't you think to read the instructions?"

"Well no, actually I forgot about that," I replied. Anyway they are all in French. We are going through the tunnel and it is the same price, you just pay for the vehicle and James gave me forty euros for petrol, so I have ear marked this for Marks and Spencer. I must get James to show me how to send a text again as I have forgotten. It is such a relief he is coming with us, or this mobile phone would be a complete waste of time.

Itchy Feet

October 10th

Our holiday in Rhodes had been relaxing, and refreshing. Next time though, I would prefer to go earlier in the season, and avoid the torrential down pours and thunderstorms. Terry wasn't bothered, not being a sun worshiper he was more than content to devote his time to the local taverna, chewing the fat with Dmitri. It hadn't been without excitement however and we'd had a spectacularly terrifying adventure. I thought at one point I might end up coming home in a box. Before our holiday, scanning the Internet an incredible plot of land that was for sale had caught my eye. Terry had said he liked the idea of building a house in Greece. So we decided we would check it out. The plot was on the opposite side of the island to our hotel, so we just had to go and have a look.

Armed with our guide books we jumped into our little, red 'Noddy' hire car and set off. Well, map reading is not one of my strong points so, after getting lost a few times, we eventually found a sign post. The alarm bells should have gone off when we saw it read 'SCENIC ROUTE'. Oblivious to the craziness of the Greek tourist board we thought, this has to be the way. After steadily climbing the mountain for two hours in second gear and fearing for our lives we finally made the summit. We were still on the 'SCENIC ROUTE' and as there had been nowhere to turn off, we had no choice but to carry on. Luckily we had not seen another vehicle, as God knows how you were supposed pass, even the goats appeared very surprised to see us. At the top we got out for a much needed toilet break and to see if we could find our bearings. We could however now see both sides of the island and were faced with the tortuous descent in front of us. I was nervous and, after spotting a little chapel in the clearing at the top of the peak, I thought it might be a good idea to confess my sins before plummeting thousands of feet to my death whilst dressed only in a swimsuit and sarong.

Our prayers must have worked as, with Terry's expert driving skills, we managed to navigate the boulder-strewn path to the safety of a tarmac road. I felt like getting out and kissing the ground - I was so pleased to see an even surface. I now knew how the Pope felt when his plane landed safely in foreign parts.

Later that night and safely back in the bar, where we would remain for the rest of the holiday, the owner Dmitri, asked how we had got on exploring the Island and had we found the other side.

Terry explained, "Found the other side, yes, and we are now fully converted members of the Greek Orthodox Church, as it was only a miracle that saved us from death today."

Looking confused Dmitri said, "I think he needs to take more water with his Ouzo, Karin."

Dmitri and Terry were hatching a plan, later when the bar closed up they were going to visit the 'house of Pink Floyd'. After all the excitement of the day I preferred to get an early-ish night so left them to their midnight expeditions and went to curl up in bed with my Jackie Collins.

The following morning I asked Terry what they had been up to.

"We drove to the 'house of pink Floyd', which was really Dave Gilmour's holiday home, he wasn't in, we sat outside the ornate gates that lead to the driveway had a nice smoke and talked about Greek politics and football."

"Sounds like I missed a riveting night," I said.

"Dmitri said they wrote Dark Side of The Moon at that house."

"They must have been up that mountain." I said seriously.

It seemed to take ages to get back to France, but James brightened up the journey by telling us about his adventures in Blighty, first he had been arrested and taken from London to Bristol handcuffed in a police car. After we nearly collapsed with shock, he explained what had happened. He had got a day's work taking down a brick wall with his cousin, but he was unaware that behind the wall was a motor home and the guy paying them to demolish it was stealing the RV. Anyway, it sounds as if it all kicked off as police turned up, along with surveillance helicopters. Someone ended up being stabbed and then they were bundled off to the nick. He and his cousin were let off as they had just been in the wrong place at the wrong time.

"Wow, James, sounds as if you had loads of excitement" we said, open-mouthed.

"Yes," he said, "and that was only the first day!"

England is truly full of amusement. Let me explain something about James, he doesn't want to be in France anymore than I do and he gave up everything to move here with his family, he is finding it more and more difficult. He is only twenty and at six foot five is also the tallest man I have seen outside the Guinness Book of Records, so his next exploit took a lot to imagine. Firstly how he did it and why he did it - surely there must have been a risk he would put his back out? He and his cousin, (this cousin was getting a lot of blame, is this why his Mum and Dad moved him away?) had been reading the small ads in the Sunday Sport - you know the ones, 'granny sex, listen to my old wrinkled pussy' and 'bored housewife - what I really get up to with the vacuum cleaner'. That sort of thing, anyway they thought let's book an escort, well when I say escort the advert meant prostitute.

So they phoned her up and she explained that she would be at junction nine off the M25 from seven o'clock onwards on Friday night, so they made an appointment and turned up. I was agog at these revelations and asked what it had been like.

"Great, really good, we did it in her car," James said.

"What sort of car did she have?" Terry asked.

"An Ford Escort," replied James

"An escort, in an Escort!" Terry laughed.

"Yes, that's right a mark two Ghia, red two door, hatch back, with a CD player and everything" added James.

"An escort, oh my God, are you serious! How an earth did you manage that? Did you stick your legs out of the sun roof?" I asked curiously.

"What did she charge? " Terry enquired.

"Seventy pounds," was the rather pleased reply.

"That's a bit steep," Terry said - the canny northerner in him coming out.

"Don't worry, I got my money's worth. We were at it for over an hour and I went first. You know I was quite surprised at how tight she was, I thought for someone on the game she would have been a bit saggy down below, you know, but she was well worth the money."

I'm so pleased he had spent his wages sensibly. I just hoped his poor mother never found out. Although, it's a shame I didn't know earlier as I could have lined him up with Annie. She could have had some decent sex and made some cash. Although they would really have been in trouble as she only has a smart car.

Anyway, at least it paled my exploits into insignificance. I had woken up that morning with little memory of the night before, Terry was soon to remind me. We had been to Annie's son's welcome home from Afghanistan and belated twenty-first birthday party. I was still operating on holiday mode so I did no more than get rip roaring drunk. I was so taken by the bevy of handsome, super-fit Marines, and I felt it was my duty as a British citizen to inform them of how proud we are of them all and how we admire their character for having the guts to do such a dangerous job. I therefore went round drunkenly telling them all I loved them and groping them inappropriately. I think I got the message across.

"You old slapper," my husband shouted at me, "you really are getting too old to get away with that kind of behaviour Karen, what on earth were you thinking?"

"I don't know, I suppose I just got overexcited at seeing so many Marines in one place. Knowing what they had been through, giving their lives for Queen and country and some of their mates being killed and wounded." I said trying to defend my drunken behaviour. "It must have been really tough on them. You see them on the TV but it's different to actually be in their company, they are so young - it sort of humbles you." I said.

"I do know what you mean." Terry nodded.

"And they were bloody fit!" I grinned.

October 11th

Home again, it was pleasant to be back, although I could have quite easily have stayed in England. It was getting harder and harder to say goodbye to the shops and Sarah. I always get this the post-holiday blues, but this time it seemed worse. I suppose it was because I realized I was going back to an empty house, once Mum and Dad had left, Terry back at work and Ashley at school all week, I would be on my own day after day - just me and the dog and he wasn't much company these days.

This time I knew I had a choice and I had finally had enough of being away from my family and friends. Enough was enough and something had got to change. Something must change, or I may end up like the previous occupant and jump off the cliffs at Granville. I was serious, when Ashley goes off to university next year I don't want to be here in France.

The only problem was how I was going to voice this to Terry. As he keeps reminding me, it is totally my fault we are here and, in fact, he has embraced it more than me and doesn't want to go back to England. He's not too keen to stay in France either, and would be quite happy wandering the planet until he drops dead. I told him he would have made a good nomad.

That is it though, when you don't have a close family you can just go where you want, do what you want - no ties, no guilt, just freedom. My Mum once said that she thought the only way she will ever be herself is when her Mum dies, and as her Dad is dead, she will then be truly on her own. She thinks that somehow by not being anyone's child anymore she will feel freer to be herself. I sort of know what she means, Terry doesn't have this feeling and this allows him the freedom to be who he wants to be, go where he wants and live where he wishes. I'm not sure if he likes it, or if it is a case of being pragmatic, just getting on with what life dishes up, but he never complains. His family is so spread out and we have not heard from some of his brothers and sisters for years, one in particular has still not replied to our wedding invitation and we have been married eleven years. His Mum is happy in Scotland and, after shoving Terry out when he was fifteen, to set up a love nest with her boyfriend she has never been around much. In fact, she keeps in touch with one of our friends she met at our wedding more than us. The drunken postman – such a lovely man - if only she knew! It is a bit embarrassing having to find out what she has been up to via them, but there you go, at least we have some contact.

Terry will not want to return to England and why should he? He has a successful business here, he has built us a stunning and spacious home, even though we still don't have skirting boards in the dining room. He has wonderful quiet roads to enjoy on his motorbike, a home cinema, cheap fags and as much wine as he can drink and Maxim can supply. What with the endless Motor Cycle News that my mum posts to him he is more than satisfied. This was going to be tough, I had to convince him we had to go back.

October 13th

Mum and Dad have left, we all got up at five o'clock to wave them off. Mum had, as usual, been busy; making me new seat cushions for my kitchen chairs, prepared jam, pickles and frozen the apples from our trees. Dad had pruned my roses, planted my leeks and painted the garden bench. He had spent hours picking up the spikey husks that had dropped from our Châtaigner tree.

"Bloody nuts! As soon as you think you have collected them all up, whoosh, and another load fall to the ground!" He had exclaimed. "Can you go on holiday at a different time next year? I'm fed up with gathering the damn prickly 'hedgehog' shells up." Poor Dad. At least he had made us an array of bird tables to entice our feathered friends.

"Your dad has had my best wood again! How many bird tables do you need in one garden?"

"He collected all the nuts though." I said defending him.

"Yeah and had a bonfire with the shells in the middle of the veg patch."

The house however was so tidy and both Terry and Ashley kept opening the fridge and pantry doors, going 'ooh, ahh' as it was so sparkling and ordered. I was rather hurt when they both asked me how long it was going to stay like that. Mum and Dad had also looked after Sam and Ashley managing not to lose either of them, which is no mean feat. I thought they had done a prodigious job. My Mum confessed that she had been lonely and the only visitors during the three weeks had been Colin, the Jehovah's Witness and Barry, an old labourer of ours, who had called by to borrow some acro props.

168

"Doesn't the solitude get you down Karen," My mum asked.

I suppose, not wanting them to worry, I had never previously admitted that it did, only moaning to Terry and the dog.

"I understand now why you always go on about moving back to England every time you come and stay," she said. "I thought you were just being silly, I mean, big detached house in France compared to a small terraced house in England, quiet roads in Normandy, total gridlock in England, working nine to five in the rat race, doing nothing in northern France."

She had hit the nail on the head. I was doing nothing, going nowhere, I had given up and retired and hadn't even joined the OAP's club. I was still a relatively young woman. This was self-imposed exile from the real world and, whereas some people thrive on this lifestyle, I was losing the plot and losing it big time.

No wonder I went so crazy on holiday - up all night, drinking thirteen cocktails in a row, telling everyone how much I loved them! I had to get my life fitted into short slots. It was as if I was two people; Karen the socialite, life and soul of the party, and Karen the recluse. I knew I didn't want to be drunk every night and make a complete fool of myself with muscular Marines, but I also knew I was fed up spending Saturday nights watching the X-Factor alone, except for the dog and a bottle of gin. I had to get a balance. God, even my mum had been bored here, and she's practically prehistoric.

October 15th

Checking my emails I had another one from the Scientology Mission in Bournemouth, apparently they are having a Dianectics seminar next month and wanted to know if I would like to part with my money. I declined their kind offer of enlightenment, preferring to spend my money on wine and fags.

Elaina and Tina, the Dutch lesbians, who live in the next commune, had phoned. Our dog's original owners, Brigitte and Wolfgang, had introduced us to them. They had initially been offered Sam, as they had a few rescue dogs, but one of these, Bruce, had just bitten the postman so they had their hands full and declined the offer. They wanted to know if Terry could build a secure dog run for Bruce, as their insurance company and La Poste now demanded this. It was either that or have Bruce shot. So they thought they would try this first.

As Tina had been a vet in Holland, she said she didn't know what all the fuss was about and you should see some of the dog bite cases over there, this was merely a scratch in comparison. The postman had to have ten stitches and now walks with a limp. They had been required to pay all his medical bills - luckily they were insured. Nonetheless they had been informed a dog pen was obligatory, and all this upset was playing havoc with their attempts to have a baby. I said I would send him round. I hoped they were just after his carpentry skills and not his sperm - knowing those two I wouldn't put it past them. Let's face it, I bet she has all the equipment necessary to perform artificial insemination. I reminded him about last January, when his first job on arrival was to assist transporting a dead Alpaca into her 'surgery' so that she could carry out an autopsy on the deceased animal.

There are some strange people living here, and for some reason they always seem to gravitate towards Terry, they just love him. He is very friendly and a good listener, but the old dears and those without a man nearby just love to get hold of him and his hammer. They tell me endlessly how charming he is, how polite and how tidy and that I am very lucky lady. I say they don't know him. He says I stopped being a customer the day I married him, so I don't get the customer-client relationship he offers and have to do the cleaning up myself.

Terry really must stop handing out our email address to all and sundry though. It is no wonder I get some strange correspondence, and I was getting fed up with the Scientologists trying to wear me down into submission with their intriguing offers of self-insight and euphoria, just by typing in my credit card number, after all who in their right mind would turn that offer down, it certainly hadn't done Tom Cruise or John Travolta any harm.

Annie was on-line so we had a chat. She said she had thought about putting the web-cam on, but she was getting dressed and was naked so probably wasn't a good idea. I proudly informed her that I now have a mobile phone (pay as you go) and have put everyone on Skype. My last phone bill was just under five euros, not bad eh! Mind you, I had been away for three out of four weeks last month.

She was off to the New Forest for the weekend with a girl friend, staying in a log cabin and planning to do lots of walking and alfresco activities. She was hoping she might meet some like-minded men who were up for a bit of 'outward bound' action. Since Paul had made it safely back from Afghanistan her sex life was on the up again – I was so pleased for her.

I was planning on slobbing out on the sofa with a bottle of wine and family size packet of crisps watching the X-Factor, I really did need to get a grip and sort my life out. My pastime of tormenting the French telephone cold-callers isn't enough fun anymore. I need to inject a little pleasure into my life, but how? What was I going to do? Did they have Center Parks in France I wondered.

17th October

It was a beautifully warm, sunshiny autumn day, I persuaded Terry to come to the beach with the dog and me. I assured him that if we kept him tight on the lead and didn't let him off we would be okay. We only live fifteen minutes away from the sea, but have hardly been there this summer. This is mainly because the dog has a death wish and we are too afraid that drowning is his preferred method.

We made it to the wide-open, sandy beach and were having a wonderful time watching Sam excitedly digging and splashing in the rock pools, when I heard shouting.

"Teeerry, Karin, Sam," I looked round and squinted - without my glasses on I could just about make out the distant shape - it was Wolfgang.

"What are you doing here?" We asked in surprise.

"I vill come to mend the shower. I am here for three days then I vill go back to Brigitte and Jenny in Germany," he explained.

Sam was pleased to see him, if a little confused that Jenny was not here. Rainer told us that they were coming to France for Christmas and that he would try to obtain a copy of the film, Dinner for One, for us to watch, as it is so funny. I must find out what this Dinner for one is, and why the Germans are fascinated with it.

October 23rd

I have now given up smoking, at last, so treated myself to a big bunch of flowers, well no one else buys them for me. Terry, being primarily a Buddhist, says he doesn't believe in cutting flowers – I, however, am not sure if that is just a good excuse to be tight. I often tell him that I don't know many Buddhists who smoke, drink and curse like he does, but he takes no notice of me.

Anyway, he may have forgotten but it is our eleventh wedding anniversary today. Bizarrely, I only married Terry on the recommendation of a tarot card reading. We had been going through a rough patch. After staying with my brother in his house in Brittany for most of the summer, Terry had been helping him to put a new roof on his derelict barn, with me assisting in paying for it. I had just sold my business and was feeling generous. We had returned home to Devon and Terry had ignored me for a week, he was living at the caravan park where he worked. I was confused by this behaviour as we had had the most wonderful time. My children had been with us and it had been fantastic, no rows, well only about having ravioli again for tea over the camp fire. It had been idyllic, calming and carefree. Anyhow, for some reason he was now giving me the cold shoulder so I was giving it back.

I decided to get away and went to see Annie for the weekend. When I told her I was coming to stay, she said that would be great as she had a woman coming round to tell her, her fortune and that Julia would be there as well. So we all had our tarot cards read and mine was worryingly accurate. She knew it all; that I lived by the coast that I had just sold my business; she informed me that I would shortly be buying a new house with sea views. She knew I was recently separated and had a new boyfriend, but we were scared of commitment, believing each one of us would dump the other, as we had both been hurt before. She told me that I was not to worry; it would all work out well. As she had turned over the proposal card, the marriage card, and finally the happy family's card – she informed me that my life was to change. I explained that I had been married twice before and had no intention of doing it again, but I couldn't resist asking her that if I did what sort of marriage would it be. She asked me to pick a card and I picked out the stars.

"There you go, that is as good as it gets. It will be a very blissful marriage if you look after each other, are compassionate to one another's needs and feed this marriage. It can't get any better, the card shows you are a match made in heaven," she informed me.

I went home to Devon, Terry proposed and we were married one month later. Oh, and we moved into a new house with amazing views of the sea. All these years later, I like to think that we truly are, a match made in Devon.

October 28th

Had a really bad week, everything always seems to come at once. The dog decided to dig up most of my lawn looking for moles then, filthy, exhausted and scared by the hunters' guns, naturally took refuge on my freshly laundered bed.

Dad phoned; he was in the dog house too. Apparently next-door cats were still fouling the back garden. Trying to be helpful he had put the washing out on the line, only to get cat shit (again) all over his slippers. He had traipsed it back into the house, through the kitchen, into the dining room and finally the lounge, before my Mum smelt it and went mad.

I asked him if he wanted to borrow Sam, he would sort out the moggy posse that was terrorising the neighbourhood with their bad toilet habits. Dad said he thought it was a great idea, that or an air rifle, but he knew my Mum would never agree, so in the meantime, he was putting down orange peel and changing his slippers before venturing in the garden.

Sarah phoned to say that she was not well. She had a bad cold, a sore throat was behind with the washing and cleaning, the flat must be really bad. I just wanted to go and help her, tuck her up in bed and give her flat a good clean, do her laundry and cook her something nice to eat. Instead I was stuck here, moping about and worrying about her wading through all that washing up and dirty laundry.

Then Mum phoned to tell me all about Dad's escapades with the cat poo. I said I had already heard all about it as he had phoned while she was out. She had been to see my Gran, who had not been well with a tummy upset. She had been very tearful and confused, which saddened Mum. Dad had lost his coupon for the Irish lottery and thought he had won twenty quid, so was tearing the house apart looking for it and making a bloody mess. What with that and the cat shit, she said she was not sure how much more of this she could take. I cheered her up by telling her about our problems, this seemed to work and she sounded a lot calmer by the end of it.

Terry was still struggling with his crazy customers. The teatime steward's inquiry was as common as the salt and pepper now. They wanted to be in their new house for Christmas, but no matter how many people had told them this was not going to happen they were blinkered and determined to move in.

"But the roof is still not on," I said to Terry.

"Yes, I know and he's asked me to build the dormers now. I have told him each dormer window will take me at least two days just to do the timber work and there are six of them. What with them and with the rest of the roof to build, we are looking at least four to five weeks work before the tilers can turn up."

It really was hard to fathom it out - was it us? Had we misled them or were we right in our initial opinion that they were clueless and insane? We had come back from our holiday to find that they had not only fitted all the other windows with no roof, erected the internal doors but they had advertised Terry's job on the ex-pat forum site ARSE. We were not surprised with the last bit, in fact we thoroughly expected to be informed that Terry had been sacked when we returned from our holiday. Communications had broken down so badly that it was impossible to work out what the hell was going on.

When we took on the work we invited them round for dinner, so that we could discuss the proposed works as they had sacked the previous builder, always a warning sign. Apparently he was constantly drunk and helped himself to their materials, I thought this was normal behaviour for a lot of builders, they obviously had not met that many.

At the time we explained that with all the luck in the world, good weather, deliveries arriving on time, James managing to get out of bed and turn up, they had NO chance of being in the house for Christmas, unless they got a team of builders in and really went for it. Terry, on his own and James labouring were hard working and good, but they were not magicians, or cowboys.

So our services were no longer required. I had seen the posting when we got home, in amongst the 'for sale everything must go - returning to England' ads was:

'Roofer wanted urgently for new build near dodge city'

'Plaster boarder wanted urgently for new build near dodge city'

Two separate adverts, so it was obvious with their tight timeframe they wanted the plasterers to start while the roof was being tiled. Not put out I politely phoned them up to see what was happening. Was Terry being sacked as no one had said a word on site and he had been back two days or were they indeed looking for more trades to jolly along the job? They explained that they did not have a bottomless pit of money and therefore were getting estimations so that they could get the best prices and if Terry wanted to put in a costing for the work that was fine, as they had no problem with his workmanship.

I reminded them that we had offered to quote for the works right from the beginning when they came for dinner, but they had informed us that they preferred to pay a daily rate. This was not normal for us, a job of this size is always quoted work, signed, sealed and on a legally binding Devis, so if we undercharge or take too long we suffer. With the customers not wanting this, a daily rate was music to our ears, it was like having a proper job and being paid every Friday night. We had been over the moon to accept their offer. Who wouldn't be? The proposal had been agreed and we had booked a long overdue holiday.

Anyway it turned out they were nearly broke, running out of money and trying to cut costs. At least I knew where we stood now. After the first week back there was no improvement, in fact it had got worse as they had now employed a stonemason working on site on the black. Well, with their strange way of dealing with Terry and this latest occurrence he was about to quit. We had, however, just received our national insurance payment demands for November and December based on the tax return I had submitted earlier in the year and to our horror, we owed the RSI nearly four thousand euros!

"Please, please stick it out, if only for another few weeks or we will be bankrupt," I begged Terry.

I knew we were in trouble when I put a tax return in we had made a profit of ten thousand euros last year, yes that's right a profit of merely ten thousand euros generates a social cost of over six thousand euros a year! What a crazy system, no wonder everyone had cash under the bed or did work on the black in France, as if you dared to make a profit you were penalised so much it wasn't worth working. Something has to change with a system like this - you are asking for trouble, everyone would be on the fiddle and indeed most were.

We would have to carry on with the work for a few more weeks or it would be prison or having the telly repossessed and no one wanted that. I broached the subject with Terry.

"What are we doing this for? Putting up with crazy, incompetent customers who could not give a damn about us, trying to run a business legally and being penalised for making a lousy profit. Putting up with being labelled foreigners, not even being able to get the same discount as the French artisans because we are English, even though we are registered with the Chambre de Métiers and pay into the same system. I have had it - ten years is plenty. We have struggled and worked hard, strained to fit in, but we will never be accepted, and you know what, I'm not sure I want to any more. I have had enough - I am proud to be English, I love my country, warts and all, she is not that bad. After ten years here in France I will accept crowded roads, I will embrace the awful politicians, the underfunded NHS. I will cringe at our football team, but most of all I will cherish that part of me that is British."

"Yeah, but I would really like to go and live in Greece." Terry replied.

October 31st

Getting back into the routine and enjoying the peace and quiet again. The countryside is truly beautiful, every time I go out in my car each turning brings more whoops of amazement. The leaves have changed colour and everywhere is a mass of oranges, reds and greens - it is certainly splendid this year, I have never seen it this spectacular before. I am not sure what it means, are we in for a bad winter? There must be some old wives' tale relating to this occurrence. My thoughts were rudely interrupted by Terry shouting me.

"Karen, what the hell have you been looking up now on the internet? My dog keeps licking his p." He carried on

"His paw," I replied. "Paw, Sam had a sore paw, and kept licking it so I googled it."

Picked Ashley up from the train station. He had been to Ireland to see Sophie. He had flown to Paris and caught the train from Paris to Villedieu.

"How was Sophie? Is she okay, does she like being an au pair?" I asked, keen for news. I had missed her not being around.

"She is fine doing really well; she's got a Mac now."

"Thank god for that, but I think she may need a warmer coat for the winter, it gets really cold in Cork."

"No Mum, a PC, an Apple Macintosh."

"Still no coat then," I asked.

"She borrowed one," he said.

"So is she speaking anymore English?" I asked

"Yes and she has learned two new words - spuds and wedges."

"Still into her potatoes then," I smiled.

Terry had been to Brittany to see Sid, my brother, as he was looking for some old windows to make a cold-frame for the garden and we were glad to get rid of our rubbish. He went off for the weekend and stayed the night. When he got back I asked if he had had a good time and how my brother was.

"Great yeah, he gave me a book Technology of the Gods, and some films to watch about subliminal advertising."

"Did you go to Tubby's?"

"Yes it was his birthday," Terry answered

"Did he get smashed or was he behaving himself," I asked. Terry knew exactly what I was getting at.

"No he didn't get drunk; he behaved himself and didn't show anyone his willy. Sid and I slept in Muppet's double-decker bus. It was unbelievable, made me feel a bit like Cliff Richard."

Laughing he carried on, "mind you, even with all that space, we still had to share a bed - I have just about slept with all of your family now."

"How's my brother is he okay?"

"Yeah he's fine, says he doesn't blame you wanting to leave France though, he's just about had enough, what with Frederic still living in his caravan and eating all his cheese, doing all that body building, and Ludo turning up all the time, talking bollocks, and playing the drums like a demented maniac, he says he's fed up."

I was surprised to hear this I thought he was happy and enjoying his rural life. Even though he still doesn't have an inside toilet.

"No, Sid says when the kids have gone he doesn't know what he'll do, without them and with only French lunatics and mad English for friends he said he would end up bonkers. What with only, Popeye and 'animal' for company, he said he can see where you're coming from."

Terry then hurried off to watch the 'alternative view' DVDs my brother had kindly lent to him. I must ring Sid and find out what Terry said, perhaps he is coming round to my way of thinking at last?

The End Is Nigh

5th November

I was still feeling down after returning from our holiday in Rhodes and brief stay in England. I just couldn't shake off the feeling that I didn't want to be in France anymore. It usually takes me a few days to get back to normal after being with my family and friends, but this time I simply could not seem to dispel my feelings of homesickness. I found it difficult to find the words to explain to Terry how I was feeling, so I decided to write him a note and let him know how I felt. I just have to pluck up the courage to give it to him, cowardly I slipped the note into his lunch box, wondering what he would think when he opened it. That night when he came home he wasn't in a good mood.

"If you took as much trouble with my sandwiches as you did with that note I might enjoy my lunch a bit more," he complained.

We had dinner and there was no mention of the note again, nothing, then he disappeared swiftly after our meal to watch Star Trek in his cinema. At least Data would cheer him up I thought. He obviously did not want to talk about it and I was therefore back to square one. I had at last broached the subject, but had been stonewalled by him. Now what was I going to do?

November 6th

I have just caught the dog with a dead rabbit on the lawn. After closer inspection it was glaringly obvious it had been dead for a while, as it was heaving with maggots. I called Terry and while I tipped a bucket of water over the dog's head, he retrieved the rabbit with a spade.

"Just think if he had brought it into the house," I said grimacing, "this dog will be the bloody death of me and you would have heard me scream all the way to Dodge City," I shouted as Terry washed his hands in the sink.

Terry was still sticking it out with his crazy customer. They had just started on the roof joists and once they were finished he would be on his way. He had no intention of quoting for anymore work and would be relieved to get away and work for our normal customers again.

"You'll never guess what he has done now," James said as he came in for his nightly cup of coffee after work, before setting off home.

"I don't know, put the curtains up?" I said, as after returning from holiday to find all the windows installed, complete with glass but with no roof, nothing would surprise me.

"He has only started to put the insulation in behind the walls."

"What, in this weather? It chucked it down all weekend and most of today, what on earth is he thinking? It will be a disaster - that stuff takes ages to dry out, if it ever does. What a complete nutter!" I exclaimed.

"It is so embarrassing, all these builders keep turning up to quote for the works and I feel like shouting that it wasn't me, I didn't put the windows in, fit the internal doors, make the stud partition walls or completely balls it up," Terry said in disgust.

"Anyway most of the guys quoting for the work look like they have been on the P&0 course. They are still driving around in English registered vehicles; half of them look inexperienced so they should get along fine. I'm out of there tout-suite and I refuse to put my name to it."

At least the teatime steward's inquires had stopped. The guy was just a crazy fool and no amount of analysis could help him, the end was in sight for Terry. Terry has a good job lined up for next week. Colin, the Jehovah's Witness, had himself witnessed much of our own building work here in Normandy over the years, and liked what he saw. He has asked Terry to build him a porch (not a church porch) and Terry had given him a very reasonable price, figuring out that as Colin visited most of the British community in Normandy at least once a month it would be a very good advertising ploy. If anyone wanted a builder then Colin could recommend Terry, and what better than having a recommendation from a man of God. Terry was so pleased with his idea, he was even thinking of asking how much it would cost to put an advert in the Watchtower.

8th November

Terry is at the Dutch lesbians today so I made him wear two pairs of pants. They had cancelled last week as Tina had managed to saw through her leg. She told me it was all mended now after being stitched up and bandaged by Elaina. She was nearly back to normal, but explained that it had been very painful and that it had been necessary for her to stay in bed for three days to let it mend. Tina had given her some painkillers and she was feeling much better. I had to bite my tongue when I wanted to retort, 'now you know what that postman felt like.'

Had to call a friend today, when I say friend, I have not actually even met her. She and her husband run a small company like us, but he specialises in erecting conservatories. Anyway, they had a contact that fitted fosse septiques and our customer needed one, so we had put him in touch with this French company. They had agreed a price, signed the paperwork and handed over a large deposit.

However, a year later the work had still not been done and our customer was getting extremely annoyed and fed up with waiting for the installation to commence. He was getting impatient with me, and I was getting impatient with the conservatory man, who would, hopefully in turn be VERY impatient with the French guy who promised to fit the fosse septique twelve months ago.

This is quite normal here, after signing a quote for work to be carried out, the artisan then has up to two years to fulfil his obligation. This does not suit the British who usually want their work completed yesterday and are not known for their patience - especially after having parted with large amounts cash. This is why we get so much work off the Brits, they all start out wanting to employ the French and it is only when they have been let down, that they contact us, explaining that they wanted to employ a French artisan. My usual reply to them is, 'well, you are in luck then as my husband is a French registered, fully paid-up and legitimate artisan – he just happens to be English.'

After I'd got my frustrations with the fosse man off my chest, we had a chat. She told me she was fed up after ten years of struggling to get by. Her husband had become seriously ill and their insurance company was refusing to pay his hospital bills, not only that, but he didn't have any work lined up for the New Year. He was therefore planning to de-register and go on the dole. They had simply had enough, their house had been up for sale since last January with no interest in it so she had finally put it on an English estate agent's web site for five hundred pounds (for the advert not the house) instead of the twenty eight thousand that the French estate agents wanted for selling it. The house was only up for three hundred thousand, so it did seem an awful lot of commission for doing practically bugger all.

She said that you can only bang your head against a brick wall for so long. I sympathized, telling her I totally understood and that in fact I'd had the same niggling doubts about staying here. The prices had gone through the roof and it was becoming just as expensive to live here as in the UK. There really was little difference, in fact you could get your shopping a lot cheaper in England now and Asda were doing a good promotion on wine, offering three bottles for a tenner. Now that I had given up smoking there wasn't even the attraction of cheaper cigarettes. She said she was amazed that the French stick it out and she was dreading the winter, it is always so depressing here. It's nice to have a chat - it does cheer me up.

Had a look at her house on the web site. We had never been invited over and despite wanting to order some windows from them for our house; they had never made it here. Something always seemed to crop up; bad weather, husband in hospital, too busy – so, for some reason we had never met. Their house was beautifully finished off (not like mine) and very neat and tidy (also not like mine). I was amazed they had not sold it. That is really depressing, knowing they have had it up for sale for over a year and no takers. What on earth would we do?

I had been hatching my big plan to get us back home. We would sell our house and have enough equity to buy two small houses in England and rent them out. Then with the rest of the money we would buy a plot of land (very small and very cheap) and build a house, whilst living in a caravan on-site. We would then sell it and do it again until we had enough to buy our own house. We would live off the rent from the two houses we had bought. Simple!

It was a good plan and I was very proud of it, we just needed a big injection of capital to get us going and that meant getting a good price for our house. If we could not do this or it took years to sell we were scuppered and would have to endure this life for far longer than I had anticipated. This would certainly push me over the edge. We had to make it saleable and find someone wanting to pay the asking price. I would have to start watching Location Location again - Kirsty and Phil would surely give me inspiration. I phoned Sarah and told her what I was thinking,

"I have waited ten years to hear you say that Mum. I want you to come home, I miss you so much," she cried.

I had missed her too and just hoped I could convince Terry. I did not want to let her down, I had missed enough of her growing up and I hated it. I wanted to see my family, twice a year is not adequate and I had no intentions of spending another ten years away from them. The clock was ticking and I had made up my mind.

9th November

After scolding the dog for digging up my garden looking for moles again, I phoned a friend who is an estate agent – well, she went on a four day course, parted with some cash and now she can value houses and sell them. I find this amazing as to register as a builder Terry and I had to go on a six week course, every Monday from nine until six, with a two hour lunch break, naturally and part with a considerable amount of money. This was necessary even though Terry presented his qualifications and I gave them my accounts from the past three years for the flats I ran, to show I knew how to do book keeping. They have some crazy rules, but there you go, it must be something to do with all that commission they get, they must give the government a backhander.

She said she would call me and come and give me a valuation. There is no point in getting all excited about my plan if it is a no go-er. I will just have to think of something else in order to get back to England.

We have been broke and had nothing before, so Terry is not keen to repeat this. He will only consider my idea if the sums add up, otherwise he is enrolling in Greek for Beginners at night school.

Terry was late home and when he eventually got in, soaked and wet through, I asked him why he was so late. He told me he had wanted to finish the job that day, so that he didn't have return to the Dutch girls the next day. It had been pouring with rain all day, so I was surprised that they hadn't finished and come home earlier.

"Was it that bad?" I asked, whilst filling the kettle to make a well-deserved hot drink for Terry and James. Terry replied, "No, not bad, just weird. I turned up and first we had to help move the bed, as Tina is still in pain with her leg and they wanted to make the room more comfortable for her. Anyway, James and I got on with it and as we moved the bed we found old knickers and a vibrator under it." James sniggered and added, "You know, one of those big black mamba ones that look all knobbly and angry."

"Yeah, I get the picture," I said cringing.

"Well, James picked it up and was holding it, when Elaina walked into the bedroom and I asked her, meaning the bed, where do you want me to put it? Well, you really don't want to hear the rest it was a bit rude and James went bright red. I felt a bit embarrassed, exposing James to that kind of sexual harassment in the workplace," he said coyly. "Anyway, it got even weirder at lunch time as Elaina had told us to come and eat in the kitchen. She had made some coffee and then proceeded to try and persuade James to become a sperm donor."

"What? Are you serious?" I asked.

"Yeah, they are desperate for a baby and James is desperate for a new motorbike, so they thought they could do some kind of swap. He said he didn't even need the turkey baster and would be up for it 'au naturelle' but I don't think Tina was keen on that."

I said I thought he should watch it; he could get in trouble if James Mum found out, she would kill him. Terry explained that was why he wanted to finish in one day and told me that if they phoned again to give them Greg Jones' number as his wife had recently left him and at least he was over twenty-one. He didn't fancy James getting caught up a tug of love, saying laughingly that it would be like something off the Jeremy Kyle show.

11th November

It has been raining non-stop now for over a week. Terry was supposed to have finished at the new build and have started building Colin's porch. Instead the work has been rained off and he is sitting in the kitchen watching Al Jazeera news, CNN, Russia Today or the new one he has found, Press TV (he doesn't trust the BBC to report everything). He is starting to get on my nerves and I asked him if he fancied doing a few little jobs around the house? To which he replied, no, he did not. I cunningly said that if we put skirting board on in the dining room it might help to sell the house, at which point he sloped off to his cinema to console himself with Deanna Troy and the rest of the starship enterprise. I hope Captain Picard can cheer him up, although I have a sneaky suspicion that he's more into seven of nine.

12th November

Sandra called round today to value the house and I was really disappointed with the figure she told me. I thought we would be able to sell it for a higher price, but, as she explained, there isn't the demand for houses of this size any more as everyone is downsizing and trying to cut down on the electric bills, not to mention the Taxe d'Habitation and Taxe Foncière - they are huge for a house like this, nearly what you would pay back in the UK. I tried to keep my composure, but I'm sure she could guess I was shocked with her valuation.

"You could put it on for more, it just might take longer to sell," she suggested.

Phoned my Mum and told her the bad news and all she could say was, "After all you have spent on it, oh, Karen, how sad."

Go on Mum, kick me when I'm down, I thought. I knew she meant well and she was right, there was no way we would get the money back for the amount of time and work we had lavished on the house, let's face it I had painted that bloody wall in the kitchen at least ten times until I was finally happy at last with the colour. She told me they had a buyer for Joy's flat and it was going through nicely, adding "shame, you could have at least afforded to buy that".

I explained that although Joy's flat was being sold at a knock down price as it needed some work doing to it and because Mum and the rest of the family just wanted rid of it I could not have lived in her home. It has been bad enough sharing this one with the ghost of a depressed suicide; I would be terrified sleeping in Joy's house after what happened to her. I would really like to get away from the ghosts, even if they are family.

13th November

Grabbed myself a bottle of wine and some nibbles as X-Factor is on tonight and then a documentary about Take That. Terry has been banished to his Cinema, so I can enjoy it in peace, without him asking if Robbie is gay or telling me how rubbish they are. Phoned Sarah and hurriedly told her to 'get those tickets at whatever cost'. After watching the documentary they had re-lit my fire - I simply had to go and see them. The camp thing must have been a blip. They were great, once again, all together and so amazing. Robbie looked wonderful; totally fit and all man, no sign of a feminine side, just pure sex appeal. We had to get tickets to see them, what had I been thinking?

Mum, phoned and said she had watched a bit of the Take That documentary but she thought they were all 'a bit gay' and that Dad thinks Robbie is the spitting image of Norman Wisdom and it puts him right off, so she watched CSI instead. She asked if Terry wanted any more episodes of Star Trek for Christmas, as she was just getting an order together for Amazon and she likes to club all the deliveries together as she hates waiting in for the post. I told her it was the highlight of my day if the postman called, she quickly replied that I hadn't seen her postman, and he scarily reminded her of a fat Elvis, with a ginger wig.

14th November

Finally I got around to telling Terry about the valuation.

"Is that all?" he said and kept saying it for about half an hour until I thought I would put my hands round his neck and choke him to death, "Well that's it then, we won't be able to afford to go back to the UK, not unless we both find jobs straight away and work full time, which would be pointless, as we would end up no better off than we are here. At least we can look at Greece properly now and see what we can get for our money, that barman Dmitri said I would get loads of work out there as a builder."

"Only in the winter months, we still have to live for the other six months."

"You could find work as a beautician or cleaning or something," he responded, looking hopeful.

"Yeah and when would I get to see my family? It is even more expensive to get flights back and forwards to the UK from there." I was starting to get angry, but knew that losing my temper wouldn't get me anywhere, so I tried to stay calm as I listened to him, however, inside I was seething. He went on, "You promised me we would move to France for ten years max, it was supposed to be a ten year plan and then at the end of it I could choose where to go next. Well, I didn't want to come here, remember, I was on my way to India when I met you and your kids, but I did, I did it for you and now I want to go and live in Greece, so why can't you come with me and do what I want for a change?"

This was just what I didn't want. I didn't want to argue about it, but he did have a point as I had just made up my mind and changed everyone's lives and it was all my fault we were here. He told me, "You have two options; come with me to Greece or go back on your own to the UK and we will split up, separate. We will sell the house, split it fifty-fifty and go our separate ways."

This was a mess, a big mess. I didn't want to live apart from Terry any more than I didn't want to let Sarah down. She had meant it when she said she had missed me and I would not dash her dreams (not a second time anyway). I didn't want to lose my husband either, and at this rate I would end up on my own and homeless.

On the bright side I would probably get custody of the dog, although I wasn't sure I wanted him, with his track record. At this point I was seriously wondering what was in it for me? Sam seemed to have me running around in circles, literally chasing my tail. My day was planned out depending on what mood the dog was in and what he was destroying, killing or digging up at any particular time.

15th November

Made an appointment at the bank as they had paid the direct debit to RSI for our cotisations and this had tipped us over the edge. We had a four thousand euro overdraft on the business account but there was no way we were going to be able to meet next month's direct debit of one thousand seven hundred euros for our social costs. We were definitely in the smelly stuff and the only way out was to borrow more money, that or go under. We were going to have to charm the bank manager and hope he would lend us some more. Okay, we didn't have a mortgage but this was the slippery slope, neither of us wanted to be in debt and we knew there were more bills to come in before the end of the year. This is where my maintenance had helped before, but we didn't have that now. All we had coming in was Terry's wages, so he would have to prostitute himself a bit longer to 'he who shall not be told' - we just hoped he didn't run out of money and then hopefully we would at least be able to afford the turkey at Christmas.

Just finished reading a lovely book, it's about a girl who cooks her way through an old cookbook and the ensuing story of her escapades. The cookbook was by an American cook who I had never heard of, but it turns out she was the American version of my beloved Fanny Craddock. She had been the inspiration for the girl to write her novel and, reading about her, she was larger than life, and a real character I could empathise with. She had lived in Paris as her husband was working for the American embassy. One thing we shared was a lack of direction; she was alone during the day and bored, so she learned to cook eventually becoming famous, taking French cuisine to the American people, even getting her own TV show. The thing that stuck out was, like a book I had read previously, they had both set up Pay-Pal accounts so that people could send them money and they could live their dreams without having to worry about earning extra money!

This must be a new thing - only Americans could be so vulgar to ask their readers for money! I couldn't believe it and you know the funny thing was that people responded to their pleas; one wanted to buy land so her friend could build a house, the other just wanted to feed her family and friends French food. I mean, in all seriousness, who would just send you money? I know that people give to charity in this way, but would you really forward your hard earned cash to someone you didn't know so they could follow their dreams?

Anyway, it got me thinking - what if I set up one of these PayPal accounts? I could ask for money. I told my husband, who said I was mad and that the only way English people would send someone money was if they had a charity set up, preferably an animal one as us Brits just love our four legged friends, "You know I think you are right," I exclaimed, "I could set up a charity for dogs, you know, the sad, emotionally deranged ones that no one else wants, the mentally impaired ones like Sam. I would love looking after and rehabilitating those poor dogs that no one else wants." I said excitedly.

"You think you know how to look after demented dogs after having Sam for a few years, do you?" my husband asked, he was obviously somewhat suspect of my ability.

"Yeah," I said, "all they really need is routine, consistency, discipline, exercise and lots of love, mainly love really," I explained, "I've watched Cesar Milan the dog whisperer loads of times and learned his skills, and I could buy a book." I was getting very animated and fired up by the idea now. "I could call it Barking Mad I said, really on a roll.

"Okay, and what do you do for money?" my husband said, always the practical one.

"Well that's it - people send it to me, you know Pay-Pal it to me. I will promise that when I have enough money I will buy premises and set up my own charity for dogs - they just have to trust me and believe I will see it through. That woman with the book raised enough money for her friend to buy the land to build her house on; she even acknowledges their contributions in the back of her book. I could do that, the captain's log I write, I could put it on Facebook or write a dog blog."

"Sometimes Karen I really do think you have lost the plot, you really are Barking Mad."

16th November

The atmosphere is awful in the house, it is not helped by the constant rain and I'm sure the dog is picking up on it; he has even stopped stealing cushions so he must be feeling bad. Terry and I just don't seem to be able to communicate with each other. I know he knows what I am thinking and I know he doesn't like it, but what do I do? Carry on living here in solitary confinement, with my friends and family miles away. The stress of having no money isn't helping the situation either, we are broke again and there seems no way out. How can we pay three thousand four hundred euros in social charges before Christmas? I wish we had not gone on holiday now, I feel sick to my stomach. They even had the cheek to send Terry, Ashley and I, a letter requesting that we go and have a free check-up at the doctors, to monitor our health as 'it is important to look after yourself and have your blood pressure checked'.

I felt like writing to them explaining that if they stopped sending out ridiculous demands for payments them our blood pressure and health would improve. Bloody idiots, frighten you to death one minute then want to monitor your well being - talk about hypocrites. I was furious and put the letters on the fire

Decided to phone my Mum and invite her and Dad over for Christmas. I needed something to look forward to and perhaps Mum would be my ally in the 'getting me back to England stakes', although I would have to warn her to tell my Dad to stop going on about living in a warm climate and how if we moved to Greece he would come and spend six months with us, you would think that would be a deterrent enough for Terry, but no, not even the thought of my Dad living with us will put him off.

Anyway, she said they would love to come, but could she let us know nearer the date as until Joy's affairs had been settled she would not be able to go anywhere, as they were broke. She asked, if they did come, could she bring my Aunt Jayne as she will be on her own.

"The more, the merrier," I replied, thinking that way I can avoid Terry and have long conversations with Aunt Jayne about Botox. I may well need this if Take That are going on tour, otherwise I will look like someone's middle aged mum in the audience and that is not the impression I was hoping to make on Robbie.

"Have you invited your brother? He has the children this year and it would be nice to see them all," she added. I replied, saying, "he is welcome to come, as long as he promises to behave himself and no political or controversial talk on Christmas Day."

"Do you want me to bring the Christmas cake, I made it in July?" - She was optimistic she would be coming then. "Will Sarah and Ashley be there? They have some great offers on down at the Asda so I will get your Dad to go down on the bus, he can get a tin of Quality Street, a tin of Celebrations and a tin of Roses, you can pay me back. Oh and the Christmas crackers, two boxes should be enough don't you think? They don't sell them in France do they? Oh, and some shortbread and do you have stuffing?"

That's it now, with every conversation until they arrived the list would get bigger until my Mum would be supplying enough food to feed the soldiers in Afghanistan but with me paying for it of course. I was wondering if I had done the right thing or should I have just booked an all inclusive to the Caribbean - at this rate it wouldn't cost much more.

Sent Annie a text to say, have a lovely time today. She is off to Taunton to see her son, Paul, get his Service Medal from Afghanistan, it must be a really proud moment for her and one she had been dreaming about for a long time. It should be two years until he will have to go again and hopefully they would have pulled out by then. She certainly wasn't going to think that far ahead, just having him back safe was enough for now.

17th November

Phoned my brother and invited him and the children for Christmas. He asked if Sarah was coming but I said I didn't think so. She had told me the last time I spoke to her that she couldn't come because she had too much work to do for Uni. After messing up last year she was taking no chances. She told me she would be spending Christmas Eve with her Dad and then visiting her boyfriend's parents on Christmas Day and Boxing Day. I had to swallow hard so she couldn't hear the lump in my throat, but at least she couldn't see the tears in my eyes.

I told my brother about Ashley applying to go to Uni and he said that he would be better off training to be a plumber, adding "students nowadays come out with enormous debt, how on earth are they expected to make responsible adults when they start off in such a mess? It doesn't make any sense, they will be hard pushed to get mortgages and if the government get their way it could be tuition fees of nine thousand a year and that would mean debts of thirty to forty thousand! Incredible, we would be breeding a generation of debt, they would either default or disappear, as how the hell could you expect them to pay all that back?"

I had to agree with him.

He thought that this was exactly the government's plan - make people liable for the rest of their lives, then they can control you. People will have to work just to pay off their student loans and have no choice, it would be life ownership. I think he has a point, how awful to dread your children going to University, as you know it will financially ruin their lives.

Anyway he said he would let me know if they would be coming, but it would be nice to have a break as he was fed up with Frederic and Ludo taking over his kitchen and his life, "Ludo has convinced Frederic that with his George Michael good looks he would make a great gay model and as Frederic is as camp as a cucumber he's all for it. So the pair of them have taken over the fridge as Frederic is now on a strict regime and Ludo's got him pumping iron like there is no tomorrow, counting the reps and sets of his exercises whilst beating blue murder out of my drum kit, I'm telling you Kaz it's a bloody nut house here."

I sympathized with him but couldn't help worrying if he will spend the whole time trying to educate us with his alternative views. What with him and Terry glued to Al Jazeera news it was all starting to look a little fraught.

Note - start to stockpile the Gin (I may need it).

The house is up for sale. We contacted Brigitte in Germany and she has put it on her website as she sells houses. It is also on with a French agent, so fingers crossed and we will see. Terry is still keen to go to Greece; he has been looking at houses for sale on Rhodes again and trying to get me excited. I feel I have no choice but to go along with it, he has been so good to me and my children all these years and now I have to support him – even if I don't like it. When I was at rock bottom he had been there for me, always urging me on to be the best person I could possibly be. He was my true friend and I must never forget that.

It hasn't been all plain sailing living here and, spending so much time together, you really get to know each other so it's easy to start pressing each other's buttons. We have had our share of rows and even had one spectacular fight - I still have the scar on my nose to this day. Needless to say a lot (and I mean a lot) of alcohol was involved as we had been to a party and finally got home at five in the morning, both of us rip-roaring drunk. We were spoiling for a fight and we had one, the mother of all fights. I think it shook us both up and I know I thought about leaving for a long time afterwards. It had scared me to death and I was just as much to blame but eventually we drew a line under it.

On the day after it happened some friends called round. I had answered the door to them, but I wish I hadn't, as I was a mess. Terry was still in bed and nowhere to be seen. I had dried blood all over my nose and make-up smeared all over my eyes. I couldn't stop crying, but they were not a bit fazed by it, not one bit, as if living here in Normandy was enough to push you to going ten rounds with your husband. They understood only too well the pressures that we were going through. They did, however, leave Normandy having found work in England and only returned to their home in France for the holidays. On one of their visits they told us how depressed they had been about the utter fruitlessness of their situation and that they had to leave for their own sanity.

No marriages are perfect, but ours was a good marriage and worth fighting for (literally) - you have to work at it. Living in France had certainly given us this opportunity because if the same circumstances had arisen in England I probably would have been on my way, but the truth is, it wouldn't have got to that. There we were, driving each other mad, living on top of each other twenty-four hours a day, seven days a week. I had nowhere to go - I had made my bed and I had to lie in it, and I am so glad I did as it was a turning point.

We couldn't continue the way we were. Financially we could not go on, we were working so hard but not getting anywhere. We were like ducks paddling madly with their little webbed feet going ten to the dozen, but staying in the same place. We had to make some changes if we were not going to starve to death or kill each other that winter. Terry was working all hours, I couldn't get a job and it was not enough as the bills just kept coming in and with Ashley to look after too we were practically destitute.

I swallowed my pride and phoned my ex-husband to ask him to cough up for the maintenance he should have been paying for the last three years. Amazingly he agreed and things started to improve, we would never be millionaires living here, but at least we would not freeze or starve to death. Hopefully we would also stop taking our frustrations out on each other.

Things did then start to improve. Terry started building his cinema, this was a sensible move and would provide an escape for both of us - who would think that Star Trek could save a marriage?

21st November

Mum phoned to say that Dad has ordered a new telly and it will be delivered tomorrow. There was nothing wrong with the old one, but after enjoying ours Dad decided he needed to upgrade and their thirty-two inch flat screen TV arrives tomorrow. It will still fit in the cabinet, as this had been the main bone of contention because Mum didn't want it on show as her lounge was small and a large in-your-face TV would not suit the ambiance of her cottage style room.

Dad just wanted to be able to read the subtitles on a larger screen; having them on was the only way they could both watch telly at the same time as, being a bit deaf, my Dad had to blast out the sound. Now as his sight was going too, he needed a larger screen to read them, well that's what he said anyway. After a week of sawing wood and fettling bits my Mum just prays it will fit, as all hell will let lose if it doesn't. Dad had disappeared the other morning and when he finally returned home, he said he had been to Hinckley on the bus.

"What on earth for?" I asked Mum.

"To get some bits for that TV cabinet from Wilco," she replied, "I ask you, He will be the death of me; I thought he might have been taken ill somewhere as he had only popped down the street to collect his Lottery winnings and pick up his library books."

She asked how I was doing and how was the house search going. I told her I was going along with it for Terry's sake. She said, "Well you won't fall off the end of the world."

I think she was putting on a brave face as Sarah had let it slip that when talking to my Mum, that she was just as excited and hopeful as Sarah that I would eventually move back to England. However, she was scared too, just like Sarah and didn't want to get her hopes up only to have them dashed again. She felt just the same way, Sarah had told her that she got upset seeing mums and daughters out shopping together and my Mum had told her that it cut her up too.

What had I done to these people? I had abandoned both of them and they had both been brave, not wanting to upset me by telling me how they really felt. I told Sarah that was it, no more lies, no more pretending - from now on we must tell each other how we feel. After all, what is so wrong about saying "I miss you, I love you, please come home"?

24th November

Spoke to Sophie on Skype today. She is still in Ireland and enjoying being a nanny. I asked her what the weather was like. At this, she fell about laughing and said it was raining but yesterday was sunny. She then added, "Oh Karen! We are talking about the weather, I am becoming English!"

When Ashley had been on the phone to her at the weekend I had asked what the weather was like in Ireland. He explained that he and Sophie don't talk about the weather and that it is a very British thing to do, French people simply don't do it.

We carried on chatting and she told me that the other day the little boy that she looks after ran off as she was collecting him from school. She ran after him, well as fast as she could go with the pram, she had the baby with her too. When she finally caught up with him at home he was standing there with his pants down and had done an enormous poo on the doorstep. She had to clean him up and put his clothes in the washing machine and said it had put her off having kids for life - I might remind her of that one day. She said she was looking forward to coming back at Christmas and I asked her what she had misses about home

"Oh my Mum's instant mash," she sighed longingly.

I asked Ashley what she meant by instant mash, he said, "You know, the stuff out of a box, you just add hot water and there you are - mashed potatoes without any peeling."

"Without any potatoes you mean, that stuff is like cardboard, are you sure she prefers that to real potatoes."

"Yes Mum she really does," he said sighing

"Well I'll be buggered," I said, "after all these years of trying to think up new recipes with mashed potato in them and worrying myself sick that she would think I was a terrible cook as I am English, she prefers her mum's instant mash. Are you sure she is really French?" I asked.

26th November

James turned up today for work, we hadn't seen him for a while as, with not much work on, Terry had laid him off. We asked what he had been up to and he said he had been watching cookery programmes and lying on the settee mainly. I asked if he meant Ready Steady Cook, but he said no it was some Chinese bird and he thought he would be able to knock up some good nosh now after three weeks of watching her each day. He would have got on well with my Grandad I thought.

"I did a few jobs for the Lesbians as well."

"Oh, that's nice Tina and Elaina?" I enquired.

"Yeah they're a right laugh them two," he smiled.

As I waved him off after paying him, I noticed he had a new motorbike. The penny dropped and I started shouting, "Terry, what the hell has James been up to?"

"I know, I know, don't scream at me, but he really wanted a new motorbike and we didn't have any work on for him, and he said he had quite enjoyed himself."

27th November

One of the farmer's cows gave birth last week. I had seen her the day before lying down and not moving much, which was unusual but as Bruno checks them twice a day I thought nothing of it as he must know they are about to calf. Later that afternoon I spotted her again, she was calving but it looked like the calf had got stuck and she seemed in some distress. I phoned Bruno immediately and pulled on my wellies and old coat.

God knows what I thought I was going to do, I was terrified of cows and had once been fired from being a dental nurse for being too squeamish. Anyway I just had to help if I could, so I waited for Bruno to speed down our drive to see to her. Since he had managed to chop half of his arm off earlier in the year, Bruno had been behaving very strangely and it was no exaggeration to say I was scared of him. He had a habit of leering at me and turning up to check on his cows just as Terry had left the house. I had taken to hiding indoors if I saw him in the garden, I felt he was not someone I wanted to be on my own with.

The cow was in a bad way and the calf was removed by tying it to a rope and pulling it out, but it was dead. The mother was weak, but still alive, so with the other cows coming to take a look I jumped back over the fence and let Bruno get on with it. That evening he bought her a bale of hay and some water. She was still off her feet, but seemed to be resting. The next day she was still off her feet and in a worse condition, she could not move. The afterbirth had not been removed from her and she really was in some distress, also the other cows had eaten her hay.

Bruno had been down to see her and I thought he would call the vet, so I left it to him not wanting to upset my neighbour. He had been doing this all his life, so he must know what he was up to,

197

even if I didn't. The next day she was still alive, but was persistently mooing soft and low. She had still not moved, so I summoned up all my courage to go into the field (the other cows were still there) and see what was going on.

I knew since that first night she had not been given any more water, so I found one of Terry's old buckets, filled it and managed to get it under the fence avoiding the electric current. She was worn out, her eyes were bloodshot and the stench from her back end was bad. She took the water and as I held the bucket for her to drink I started to sob, there was no way this cow would make it, well not on her own with no help - she was just being left to die. I was furious, how could anyone do that?

I climbed back over the fence and called my Mum. Sam, who had picked up on my emotions, nuzzled me as I dialled their number. I just broke down, with big sobs punctuating the tale of this poor animal. I had seen her day in, day out for the last ten years, through winters and summers. I had seen them calf every year and fed them my grass cuttings when I mowed the lawn. They had been part of our lives. There were six of them and as they were usually pregnant or nursing their offspring, they were gentle and placid, I was still scared of them though, they are really big.

My Mum explained there was nothing I could do and begged me not to go back in the field, as it would only upset me even more. She advised me to wait until Terry and James came home and ask them to go in with me to see her. I couldn't wait, it was tearing me apart. She was still mooing and I had to take her some more water, if that was all I could do I would at least do that. I shut the dog indoors as I did not want her distressed any more than she already was and Sam likes a bit of afterbirth, as we found out last year, much to our disgust. I gave her the water and I swear she smiled at me as I patted her head and left her a little more comfortable, I like to think.

Within half an hour Bruno turned up on his tractor and I was having none of it. I wanted to know what was happening to this poor creature and marched into the field to get some answers. His wife was with him and between them they had tied the unfortunate beast to the tractor and were trying to get her on her feet, but she was slipping in the mud and going nowhere.

I said I thought she was worn out and told them about the buckets of water. His wife said the cow had wind and that is why she would not get up. I thought that perhaps if they had tried to remove the afterbirth two days ago it might have helped and surely a shot of something from the vet could have eased her pain. They said there was nothing they could do and would have to put her to sleep. I tried to swallow the tears as I did not want them thinking I was a softhearted English animal lover, even if I was. At least she would not suffer anymore, so I bade them bonsoir and left them to inject her.

Terry came home and found the dog and I curled up in Sam's bed. I was still crying, I just could not understand why they had let her suffer and die. If only they had done something sooner, instead of leaving her in full view of my kitchen window. It was like that scene in The Beach, where a shark attacks the guy and they refuse to get him help. They then remove him so that they don't have to witness his moans and see him suffer. The following morning the cow was still lying in the same spot, the injection must have worked and they would be picking up her body later today I thought.

"She is still alive," James shouted as they were getting ready to go to work that morning.

"What did you say they gave her?" Terry asked me.

"It was a pink liquid in a big syringe, I didn't see him inject it but he said he was going to and that she would die - 'mourir' he said, to die, that's right isn't it?"

"Well she's not dead, she is still with us. Her ears are moving and look, she just moved her head."

Thank God, she was going to make it, she was tough and was going to get through this. I smiled to myself. An hour later Bruno turned up with the tractor and he tied her to it with ropes and a chain to her leg. I thought he was going to have another go at getting her up on her feet, but instead he dragged her the length of the field into the cornfield and up to the lane. He must be taking her to his farm I thought.

I decided the coast was clear and put on my wellies and coat to take Sam for a walk. With the sick cow in the field I had not let him off his lead as I was scared he would torment her, so he was overdue for a walk. We got to the top of my drive and I knew something was wrong as all the cows from the field opposite were gathered looking at something.

There she was, she had been left there -still breathing, still clinging on to life, what could I do? I had seen the Parisians, who own a holiday cottage at the end of our road, yesterday so I would take Sam and ask them if they could help me find out what Bruno was playing at. Being French themselves I thought it would sound better than some hysterical English woman demanding to know why he was mistreating his animals and I was shit scared of him if the truth was known.

They weren't in, but luckily the other English owners had arrived, so I knocked on their door and before I could explain I started sobbing. After coffee and them having a little sniffle too, Dennis said he had to go to the bakers so he would check out the situation. On his return he confirmed that she was still there and alive. They kindly asked me to stay a little longer, sooner than have to walk by her again and go home to an empty house. After my second coffee I said I really must go and thanked them for being so kind. As I got to the top of my drive I could see she had died and there was now a small river of blood seeping its way into the muddy earth.

Tinsel, Tantrums, Tin Foil and Turkey

1st December

Mum phoned and I told her all about the dead cow, never did find out what happened to her. Terry thinks the farmer bashed her head in with a hammer or cut her throat as there was too much blood for a gunshot. I vowed never to speak to that man again and re-named him the butcher of Beauchamps.

Mum had been to see Gran, who was huddled up warmly in bed with her bright red bed socks protruding from the bottom of her dishevelled blankets. Her feet were fighting for space with her cuddly toys and an opened box of Thornton's chocolate selection. It appeared that she had tucked in, as half of the chocolates were missing and the rest had been half chewed and clumsily replaced. With her grey curls peeking out under the blankets, she had slipped down the bed yet again and with her painted fuchsia pink fingernails, Mum had found her clutching onto the padded sides of her bed as if her life depended on it.

"I just about managed to rescue her and straighten her out again." Mum said. Poor Gran, I couldn't help wondering how long she had been left this time, all scrunched up and holding on to her cradle, terrified that she would fall out. Mum went on to explain that there had been some problems at the care home. One of the carers had been hiding Gran's buzzer so she couldn't reach it and she was generally being spiteful to Gran and the other residents. They asked my Mum if she knew anything. Gran had told Mum that she was reluctant to blow the whistle for fear of what might happen to her.

"It's a bloody disgrace! This woman should be sacked immediately, how can I leave her there knowing this cruelty is going on? Do me a favour and shoot me when I'm old, I don't think I want to get like that." Mum said.

Denis called round and asked if I wanted to go shopping with his wife, I think he was trying to cheer me up as, after the cow incident, I had been a bit down in the dumps. I told him I would love to. It will do me good to have some company, even if the shops are rubbish. It never ceases to amaze me, where do the

French do their shopping? The large supermarkets are fantastic, huge and clean with wide aisles and everyone that comes to stay, loves to go and have a look around, always commenting on how spacious they are. They don't go in for shopping malls in Normandy, the nearest is an hour and half away and consists of six shoe stores, one pet shop, a stationery outlet and Toys R Us.

When I arrived back home Mum phoned again to say she had just popped into Leicester and managed to get a family size Pork Pie, along with more Christmas presents, – oh, how I'd love to go Leicester shopping. It had actually become one of my recurring dreams, I told her unashamedly that Marks and Spencer's was now one of my night-time fantasies and had relegated Sean Bean (Aye lass) to third place. Robbie, naturally, was still number one. She had bought my brother's daughters loads of knickers and tights from Primark for Christmas.

"They are so cheap I couldn't help myself you know, and such good quality, considering they are all made in Taiwan."

I didn't like to spoil it by telling her that my brother was not keen on these cut-rate clothes shops, knowing that in order to be able to sell them at rock bottom prices, some poor kid in a foreign country was doing a twelve hour day for fifty pence. She had decided not to go over the top this year on the present front (Yeah right!) as she and Dad were still waiting to hear about the sale of Joy's flat. It was taking so long that she was fed up with the whole business. I commented that it was like something out of Dickens Bleak House, Jarndyce v Jarndyce where the solicitor's fees were so extortionate there was nothing left for the benefactors. This didn't go down too well.

Anyway, until it was sold and the inheritance divided up she was broke. Mum and Dad had paid out all the expenses, but would only be reimbursed when the sale was complete - in the meantime they had to be patient. The irony of all this was that, although my Mum has Power of Attorney for my Gran, as she is still alive, Gran will get a share of the estate along with about fourteen other relatives. However, my Mum will only receive her expenses. My aunt Jayne would get a full share and my Mum was fed up with my aunt telling her what she was going to do with the money; visit a friend in California, go and see Cliff Richard (again), get a new forty-two inch TV (she had seen my Dad's) and she thinking of having have more Botox.

Mum said if she mentioned how she was planning to spend her inheritance one more time she might have to slap her. Mum had had a good look around the shops; she had left Dad watching the racing at Kempton Park on the telly as he was too slow, with his arthritic foot and she wanted to be in and out, SAS shopping. Leicester was wonderful and they always make such an effort with their Christmas decorations - I suppose the council not wanting to be out done, had to keep up with the display put up earlier in the month by the Asian community for the Diwali, Festival of Lights. I love Leicester - I once took my son there and, as we sat in a cafe watching the world go by, he exclaimed "You can see all races and nations walking by this window."

"Welcome to Leicester," I proudly said, "home of cultural diversity and tolerance, the world could learn a lot from here." I told him.

Mum carried on, "I've been on the market and got two caulies for a pound and some nice Red Leicester, so I'll make Dad a cauliflower cheese for tea. There are some great bargains about Kaz." I bet there are I thought. "I bought some lovely, purple sparkly beaded material off a nice old gentleman on the market, that will look marvelous on your dining room table for Christmas. I think it's supposed to be for a Sari, but he didn't speak much English, let me have it for a fiver, anyway it won't matter will it?"

"Did you go in to Laura Ashley?" I asked, as I knew they had a sale on - I had seen it on the TV the night before. "No, I came home as I was bursting for a wee and couldn't be bothered to go all round the Haymarket to M&S. There was a park and ride bus waiting, so I jumped on - you know, before the kids come out of school, otherwise you can never get a seat and they rarely offer one to us pensioners. The little buggers - I blame the parents," she moaned.

2nd December

Sarah phoned. She was a bit down in the dumps too. She had been contacted to say they didn't need her on Deal or No Deal after all. She said she thought it had something to do with the fact that she lived in Notting Hill and they thought she didn't need the money. It was a shame, as she was really looking forward to being famous.

Took the dog for his walk (still blood at the top of the road) and, as I had my wellies on, went round the fields gathering holly and mistletoe. However, I only managed a small amount of mistletoe, I will have to get Terry or Ashley to help out, as some tree climbing may be required.

Everywhere was fresh and warm (for the time of year) and as I walked through the fields it was so peaceful. Even the birds looked to have taken the day off, here was no hustle and bustle of Christmas shoppers, no rushing around trying to buy your presents and get the last Christmas pudding from Waitrose. Most people would breathe a sigh of relief to be away from all of that, but you know, in the middle of the field - just the dog and me, well I sort of missed it.

I had read a few books that ex-pats had written about moving to France, the upheavals, and scrapes they got themselves into. Getting to grips with the French language, going into the shops asking for a pipe, which in French translates as a blow job, yes I had done that a few times before my slip of the tongue was pointed out by my sex mad neighbour, who started unbuttoning his overalls thinking he was on to something, when I informed him I wanted a 'grosse bite of his field' (a large cock in the field!).

The trials of employing the French Artisans, yeah I knew all about that. The crazy drivers who are either right up your backside or driving like a nun on acid, slow and frighteningly erratic.

On one occasion a ninety year old, one armed man had reversed into my car and swore I had no right to be driving, mainly I think, because I was English and had no place to be here in Normandy, but I think it also had a lot to do with the fact I was a woman. He was racist and sexist, but I did wonder if he was right - what the hell am I doing here?

These ex-pats had written about their experiences and, yes, they were very funny but the point was they didn't moan, they didn't express regrets, nobody wanted to pack up and get the next boat home. I wasn't ashamed that I missed the rat race or that I worshiped the shops, that I craved a Pasty from Gregg's or that I didn't fit in. I was not too proud to admit that I had got it wrong.

Logically there had to be others out there that felt the same twinge of pain at seeing an advert for Asda or Waterstones proclaiming three books for a tenner. Life in rural France is about as glamorous as high heels on a rugby pitch, and not that cheap anymore. You certainly can't get three books for a tenner in the supermarkets I go to and the last time I treated myself to a copy of Woman and Home it cost me six euros ninety five - nearly a fiver for a magazine, Terry would have wept. The ex-pats however love a bit of Brit bashing, 'England is going to the dogs you know, full of immigrants (not sure what they think they are here in France?); the NHS is falling apart; it took six months for Norman to get an appointment for his hernia! Six months - I ask you, you wouldn't get that in France. You can't go anywhere without having to pay to park now you know, it's all traffic and rush-rush rush.'

It didn't help that if you listened to the English news broadcasts, you would think the place had fallen down. I am sure the only reason the majority of English feel more content in a foreign country is:

1. They don't watch French news or read a French newspaper

2. They don't speak enough French to understand the political situation and what the governments are up to anyway

3. They prefer to watch the BBC and have more knowledge about what is going on back home than half of the population of the British Isles

FACT - the further away from your country you go the more patriotic you become.

Note the amount of satellite dishes on British houses in Normandy all facing towards the Astra 2 signal

I have come to the conclusion that the reason most people are having a good time here and enjoying it so much is that they don't have a bloody clue what is going on, or they are too drunk most of the time to care. Lots of my friends had returned home but they had always given the excuse that it was because they had run out of money and couldn't find work, not that they craved a little excitement, that it was boring here or that they were secretly relieved when it had all gone tits up. They would pack up and leave for the ferry with comments like, 'oh you are so lucky living here, and you have made it work. I wish we could have. I do envy you.' Were they kidding themselves? Were we all just so caught up with 'living the dream' that we had lost the plot?

So the next time I was at the hairdressers I decided I would try out my theory on a few acquaintances, no friends now, they really had all gone back to England. "I don't know what you mean dear. You can get Marks and Spencer to deliver now over the Internet and the range of English goods in the supermarket is simply astonishing," commented one lady who was having her roots done and was sporting a plastic bag on her head.

"Life is soo stress free here. Don't you think so Sissy?" her companion chirped in.

"I can grow my own veg, I've got an enormous compost heap and Cyril has enough room to keep twenty chickens and a pig. I couldn't do that in Surbiton." Added the thick set, gold adorned woman, kitted out in a mauve twinset, stiff uncomfortable looking corduroy skirt, tan brogue's complete with green Barbour jacket on the back of her chair, who waiting with turbaned hair to have her tight perm combed out, looking to me more like a fat Buddha, than someone adept with a pitch fork.

"If you fancy some night life, there is an amateur performance of Jesus Christ Superstar at the Salle des Fêtes on Friday night," the hairdresser informed me.

"Oh that sounds good," I said, my spirits lifting. "I like a good sing song and I know all the words to that one."

"It is in French and there's no singing," she added.

It really was just me then. Oh they all had a good moan about the appalling driving habits of the Normans, renowned to be the worst in France, the lack of curry, dreaming about shopping malls, but no-one wanted to change, no-one wanted to go back, they were all really 'living the dream'.

Then I hit the nail on the head and asked my hairdresser, "So Liz, what if your children weren't here, what would you do then?"

"Oh, in that case I would go back, no questions asked," she replied, quick as a flash.

"I couldn't stick it here without them," she added.

That was it. If you had family and they were with you that was great. If you had family and you weren't that bothered about seeing them great, but if you had family and you missed them then you were up shit creek. Realistically you might as well be on the other side of the world, it was only five hours away (on a good day), but that was too far when you just wanted to pop in for a cup of tea and a chat. Surely even the biggest compost heap in the world cannot compensate for that.

At least now I knew what I had to do, but how did I tell Terry? I thought about it, I thought about it a lot. When I was out walking with the dog my mind would race with all the scenarios of what to say. I knew I wasn't being honest with myself but I just couldn't do it, I couldn't bring myself to be the baddy and be the one to spoil his dream of moving to Greece, not when he had let me try mine. So I vowed to try and look on the bright side - all that sun and my Dad coming to stay for six months at a time what could be better! But it was only a question of time, I knew I was kidding myself and you can't fake it forever.

3rd December

Sarah phoned, she was in the middle of her dissertation for Uni and she needed a break so decided a nice cup of tea and a chat would recharge her batteries. She asked me what I was up to. I didn't like to tell her I was hiding from the creepy farmer who I now thought was stalking me. As I had witnessed his murder of the cow I was sure I was next on the list. She had not even started her Christmas shopping yet. I warned her not to speak to her Gran in that case; otherwise she would feel really inadequate. She was looking forward to having a rest and just slobbing about watching TV and eating. I said that was the best bit about Christmas – well, that and being able to have a drink at eleven in the morning without being accused of having a problem.

She and her boyfriend have decided to spend Christmas in England and I do understand what she means when she feels it is sometimes just too far to come. She has been working so hard at Uni and her job, she just needs a break doing nothing and relaxing, not traipsing over to Normandy. I couldn't tell her how much I would miss her.

We have a customer that had sold his house in England, given up his successful business, sold all his furniture and after buying two houses in Normandy they were set to come here with his wife and start again. The plan was to rent out one house whilst renovating the other. His lifelong dream was about to come true and he would own his own small farm. Terry had quoted for the work and was due to start the following month, when out of the blue the client had emailed (easier to convey bad news in the modern world) - they would not be coming to France after all as his wife had changed her mind.

We could not believe it. They had sold everything, given up everything and he was devastated. After I had reassuringly emailed him back to say no hard feelings for stopping the work and cancelling our contract (another cold winter beckoned!) He phoned me. He was a man bereft it was awful talking to him, he sounded broken and totally crushed. His dreams that he had held dear for so long were over.

Terry and I could not understand how they had got so far, only for his wife to change her mind. Surely he would blame her for this, how do you move on from the fact that she had abandoned his dreams. He was a dejected man, would their relationship survive, how could it, we speculated?

Months later they came to visit their property. It had taken a lot to do this as his initial reaction was to sell it all and, indeed, he had put the houses up for sale. Anyway, six months down the line they arrived and we invited them for dinner.

Time is a great healer and they were looking relaxed and very happy with each other. I asked him how they had got over the bombshell and managed to carry on (what I really wanted to say was 'why didn't you divorce her for shattering all your dreams?').

He calmly explained that there had always been a clause agreed in their plan that if either one of them changed their mind it would not be too late, even if it was on the boat coming over he would understand. Wow, I was amazed - what a credulous relationship they had. I was in awe at their understanding and compassion for each other.

"What changed your mind then?" I asked his wife.

"The children," she replied. "They may be in their twenties now, but I just could not bear it and as the time for the move became closer I realised I just could not leave them. I love my husband, but without the kids I am not complete – I feel they are the other bit which makes me whole," she candidly explained.

As I sat listening, my heart went out to her and I was full of admiration that she had been strong enough to stand up for what mattered to her - her family. I knew now why her husband had accepted her decision, he had tremendous respect for her, her feelings and, most of all, he got it, he understood the love a mother has for her children and the special bond they share. He certainly would not break that, however hard it was for him.

6th December

Dropped Ashley off at school, whilst being chased by speeding motorists desperate to meet their death. The driving conditions were terrible this morning with a thick blanket of fog seeping in from the coast and engulfing the bocage.

I was driving in pitch black and you just can't see what is in front of you as there no street lights on the main road nor are there any cat-eyes. As I sped out of Granville trying to keep up with the traffic, an owl collided with my car. I saw it clearly - a white barn owl smashed into the wing mirror of my Land Rover, immediately I was jolted back to reality and slowed down. What was I thinking, driving like these crazy people? You could hardly see your hand in front of your face, but they didn't care - they were on a mission and even the bad weather conditions would not deter them. I had got caught up in their madness, but luckily the poor bird had brought me to my senses.

I was still recovering and driving much more slowly when I saw a figure in the road. I was just coming up to the dual carriageway and would have sped up again if I had not hit the owl and still been shaking - it had struck with such a bang that I was convinced I had killed it and was beside myself, worrying that I had injured such a beautiful creature.

The figure in the road was waving a torch, so I put my hazard lights on and slowed down even more, causing the traffic behind me to break abruptly. They were all desperate to overtake me and roar down the dual carriageway, but they couldn't overtake at that point and had no choice other than to sit patiently behind my vehicle. Finally, at last realising something was wrong; the cars in my rear view mirror put their hazard lights on and thankfully stopped weaving around trying to overtake. As I got closer I saw there were more torch lights and a few vehicles had stopped. There was a pile up in the outside lane of the carriageway and I could hardly believe it, a dead horse was lying in the road. It must have escaped from its field. The poor creature must have wandered onto the highway confused by the fog and with the obscured visibility, and had been hit. It had only just happened and the Gendarmes or Pompiers hadn't yet arrived.

There was nothing I could do and enough people had stopped already to assist. I carried on home thanking my lucky stars as, if I had not slowed down after the owl incident, I would have been in danger of ploughing into the accident. By now the dawn was breaking and when I arrived home I examined my car for damage from the impact with the owl. There was not a single scratch, nothing, no marks, zilch.

7th December

I called into the Noz discount store, managing to avoid some rather loud Brits in the first aisle squealing with excitement, I was looking for some more fairy lights - they had loads for two euros each so I bought four sets. It will look like a fairy grotto by the time I have finished. I shan't tell Terry I bought the lights from there as they sell end of line stock and he may make me take them down thinking they will burn the house down.

Mum phoned. She had received a letter from the Council about Gran to say they were sending someone to do an evaluation of her because she is in a bed with the bars on all the time. Apparently this was classified as an infringement of her civil liberties and therefore had to be checked out with an eight-page questionnaire to make sure her 'civil liberties' were not being infringed.

My Mum was furious, "what the hell do they think they are playing at? If the bars came off she would end up on the floor, then they would end up being sued for neglect". She definitely had a point.

She said she was also in a bad mood because she hadn't got much sleep last night. My parents live in a semi-detached house and the girl next door has a new boyfriend. "They were "at it" all night and then again at five in the morning," my mum exclaimed, "no wonder her dad came up to take the children to school, I bet she's worn out. I wouldn't mind," she carried on, "but this is the third boyfriend we have been submitted to hearing her have sex with and she only moved in six months ago." She said she had finally banged on the wall shouting 'give it a rest!' before waking Dad up to put the kettle on. Dad luckily was deaf as a post and had missed the entertainment.

It did get me thinking though, I am the same age as the 'girl' next door and it sounded like she was having more fun than I was. It was time to inject something, anything, into our relationship. We might be tormenting ourselves with the uncertainty of our future but that was no excuse for a lousy sex life.

I decided I would inject some magic back into our marriage, but first I needed to phone Annie for some ideas. When I finally got through to her she sounded a bit upset, so I asked her what was wrong. She told me she was not well, having had awful hot flushes at night and was worried sick. I told her it was the menopause and not to worry, as it was perfectly normal at our age.

She said she thought she had some terrible disease and was about to die, but asked how come I knew so much about it. I told her I had been going through it with my Mum for the last decade, depending on when she was either on or off her HRT. It was all quite normal and unfortunately we were now entering the dreaded lack of oestrogen zone that is the curse of many a woman, but it's usually over and done with in ten years.

"Ten years?" she shouted, "bloody years of no sex and hot flushes. How the hell do we get through this then? I haven't got a bloody husband and now I'm menopausal. I might as well shoot myself. I'll never have a decent sex life again," she wailed. I reassured her by telling her that, on the contrary, you can still have a sex life and, looking on the bright side, we wouldn't have to worry about getting pregnant any more. That just about did it for her; she started to howl that she wasn't sure if she was ready to give up on the idea of never having another baby. She really was in a bad way, because for years we had congratulated ourselves on being younger mums and having a life of our own. With our kids grown up we were still relatively young and it had been great; no ties and still nubile enough to have a life without attending nativity concerts, sleepless nights and catching nits.

"It can make you feel quite horny and sensual," I suggested, trying to reassure her. I'm not sure if that last bit is true, but I couldn't bear her to suffer like that. In the end I didn't ask her about how to spice up my own love life, it would have been like rubbing her nose in it.

9th December

Woke up to an almighty crash - Sam had managed to knock the Christmas tree over. "I told you it was a bad idea to put those chocolate Santas on the tree," Terry gloated as he went back to bed, leaving me to deal with the mess and a chocolate induced hyped up dog. Shouting down the stairs, he said "Anyway I thought chocolate was bad for him, you better make sure he can't get anymore, Wolfgang said it would kill him." We live in hope I thought.

Found a great article in my Woman and Home magazine - it was all about passion breakers and makers, this was exactly the help I needed. After reading through all the usual advice, comprising; not a good idea to leave your underpants on the floor (they must mean the man), not buying your wife an iron for her birthday (again the man) and eating with your mouth open. All the turn offs were definitely coming from the men, what did us women need to do then? Apparently we need to be spontaneous, tactile and ready to go at it at any time, any place. Their expert concluded that if you followed the following list you couldn't go wrong:

surprise each other

be intimate

get involved

have fun

This was good advice and I thought I had the answer! I would surprise Terry by ordering a costume the same as the character, Seven-of-Nine, wears in Star Trek. He had confessed to me that in her skin-tight costume she was a real eye pleaser and a bit of a turn on. This would be genuinely intimate - have you ever seen what that android looks like? It leaves nothing to the imagination. This would also cover point two, as I was definitely getting involved - he loved Star Trek and we would certainly have fun – point four!

Excitedly I put my magazine away and Googled Star Trek costumes, got my credit card out and ordered it. Delivery would be within eight to ten days, so I now had to think how I would arrange this surprise, oh, and go on a diet.

Friday 10th December

Had a card from Alana and Les. I think it was supposed to be a snow scene of the village where they live with Alana in a Father Christmas outfit in the foreground, and Stonehenge in the background, it looked like Les had photo-shopped it on his computer. Then again it could have been a polar bear or Alana in a full-length mink coat, standing in a quarry, who knows? It was emblazoned with the bizarre message, 'Greetings from Salisbury to all our customers!'

Anyway they asked if I would call in to their house and make sure the water was turned off and put some mouse poison down. Finally they wished us a merry Christmas and said they would see us again in the spring.

Had a look on ARSE for things for sale - looking for another mattress for the Christmas guests. Couldn't find any, but someone had a nice set of champagne glasses to sell, some serving plates and tablecloths - all very cheap. They are selling up as they had finally sold their house and were leaving in the new year, so I will go to have a look tomorrow at their 'everything must go - house sold, returning to England' sale.

Went to visit the wife of a fellow builder that Terry had met, who was thinking of moving back to the UK. After chatting on the phone about some work related query, I realised that we were both in the same boat and we agreed to get together. I also secretly hoped her husband might persuade Terry that going back to England was a good idea.

They told us all about the problems they had that weren't that different from our own and we commiserated together realising that, like them, our commune had not included them in their list of artisans living in the village, everyone else had a listing except us Brits. They had never employed them, obviously preferring native French builders rather than taking the risk of employing an English builder. Even their closest neighbours, who they thought were friends, had failed to trust them and had their roof re-tiled by a French company. They then had the cheek to ask his advice about the shoddy workmanship when the roof started leaking. His wife was, like me, bored stiff and asked me what I did to keep sane. I told her about my writing and how I escaped by letting my thoughts spill out onto the page.

She told me she had some stories for me. I have found that, like a doctor at a party who suddenly gets hassled by personal medical queries, when you tell anyone you write, they immediately want to tell you their anecdotes, how they could write a book and have loads of interesting stories to impart.

She told me how they had been so hard up earlier that year they had taken a job to dig out a fosse septique, for a customer. With no mains drainage a waste disposal system with intricate trenches and a labyrinth of pipes was required to take the sewage away from the house and into the giant storage tank, with the grey waste filtering into the surrounding field. He had paid them in full and this had allowed them to clear all their debts, buy some central heating fuel and re-stock the fridge, but it meant they had no money for labourers and only enough to hire a mini digger for one day.

This meant they had to do the rest by hand, with them both working hard in the snow and freezing cold. When her husband had tripped over and the snowflakes were beginning to fall again she had started to laugh, she simply could not stop. She laughed and laughed. With the cold snow evaporating on her flushed face the laughter turned to tears as she started to cry with great big uncontrollable sobs, they had hit rock bottom, literally. Sitting there in the freezing snow, six foot underground, they knew it could not get any worse than this.

The mood of the evening was lightened when she declared she too had written half a book, impressively informing me that erotic literature was her forté. She had jotted down some notes years ago and I persuaded her to take it up again. I have a sneaky suspicion that she will end up with a best seller, as women just love reading about sex and, as we all agreed, they are so much fonder of reading about it than actually doing it.

11th December

Went to have a look at the 'everything must go sale' and bought the champagne glasses. The serving plates were a bit 'busy' and the tablecloths had hunting scenes on; not a good idea, as my brother is a vegetarian and might be offended. They had some good books and Terry managed to get a new kettle for work.

The couple who were selling up had been here three years, and despite fully renovating their house, only got what they paid for it but, with the euro being strong against the pound, they were still coming off top and had no regrets. They philosophically said 'we tried it and it didn't work out'.

"Why didn't it work out?" I asked, being nosy.

"Oh you know, the usual - ran out of money, we couldn't find work, the wife missed the shops. You can't get a decent pint or loaf of bread and we both missed the family," they sighed in unison.

"You don't realise how much you miss your family and friends until they are not around," she said, "they say they will come and see you and they do, but that is hard too - it isn't enough, it's all or nothing here and I can't handle that. I just want to pop in for a cup of tea and a chat or go out for the day shopping, not spend the whole week having to lay on the entertainments and be a hotel manager. I'm too old for that. "

Ah, a woman after my own heart at last - I wasn't the only one. There is a fine line between spending a few hours in someone's company to them turning up and spending the week with you. We knew this to our cost. Our friend, the drunken postman, once came to stay with his partner and, as we had a house full, they camped in the garden. They had a great time and spent most of it drunk or getting drunk, falling over their tent or cursing one another and for some reason his partner insisted on hanging her very brief briefs all round the garden, this was before we had the dog.

After the fourth day I had had enough and told them so. We had a bit of a row. I tried to apologise, but the harm had been done and they have never been back. We do still keep in touch and he phoned last week to wish us a happy Christmas. We had a lovely chat and he even acknowledged that he and his girlfriend are not the best house guests, even telling us that on a birthday trip to see Mika at the Eden Project they had been thrown out of the bed and breakfast they were staying in, for shouting and swearing and being a nuisance to the other guests. He said it was a shame as they had booked for two nights. They are really hilarious couple but there is only a small window when you can enjoy their company before they are too drunk and crazy.

I first met the postman when I had just moved to North Devon. I was returning from a night out with Annie, as we walked along dog shit alley on to the high street, we witnessed him flying through the launderettes plate glass window. We pointed him out to the police as the guy who had been pushed. It was not difficult to identify him as, with his chiselled good looks and impressive sideburns, sleeveless white vest and as he always rode a cow horned 'sit up and beg' bicycle, he was quite a sight around the town and everyone recognized him.

He was also a pain in the neck and could annoy anyone. Terry once punched him in our local pub. Half the bar got up and applauded the other half offered to buy Terry a drink. Despite all of this he is quite a personality with a heart of gold and I miss his madness. In a normal town he would have stood out, and he did to a certain extent, but this was a town full of characters. It seemed to attract a different sort of person, there were actors and dancers, musicians, photographers, artists and circus performers - a myriad of talent all on the dole, signing on and drawing their unemployment benefit, whilst waiting for their big break. Locally it was known as the glue pot, as once you lived there it was very difficult to leave.

The town was set on the breathtakingly beautiful North Devon coast, but it had had its day. There were countless old hotels boarded up and going to rack and ruin, it was in a sad state and, despite the tourists still coming to visit, there was no money to rescue the place and restore it to its glory days. It was so sad to see, no work led to no money, which meant no regeneration to the once magnificently beautiful seaside resort.

Without the stunning natural landscape it would have been a very desolate place, but when the summer came, with the sea as it's backdrop, the place burst into life and shone once again. This led to a kind of carnival atmosphere and with so many out-of-work performers and artistes with nothing to do, many a happy evening was spent with campfires on the beach with the wondrous entertainment they would provide.

We were also blessed with numerous music festivals, and because Terry was friends with everyone, we always had free tickets and would finish the evening joining our mates who had been performing. At one particular event we ended up in a marquee with a dozen of the local performers who had found a barrel of beer and as we were all camping there, the party was not yet over.

One of the artists we knew well was an illusionist who went by the name of 'Zane McVain of TV fame'. He was a cross between a young Oscar Wilde and the Child Catcher from Chitty Chitty Bang Bang. He specialised in juggling with knives and fire and, on this occasion, had decided that he would show us what he was made of. He persuaded the drunken postman to lie down, only he was stupid and drunk enough to do this, and then started his act. As the postman lay himself down, his girlfriend threw herself onto his body to protect him whilst proclaiming her undying love and pleading with him not to put himself in imminent danger. It was like a scene from Hamlet, in the flickering light within the canvas tent, her long golden hair draped over his body, she looked like a dead ringer for Ophelia. His clothing askew and with a hellish look on his face, he pushed her to one side and announced he was ready, urging Zane to make haste before she could straddle him again.

Zane started his act - he was to traverse the length of his victim's body whilst juggling three ten-inch sabre-like knives. Well, the marquee erupted! His girlfriend was by now quite beside herself, loudly singing bawdy songs about death and lost love. She handed out rose petals, which she had picked from the walled garden earlier in the day, drunkenly talking in riddles and trying to engage the audience in her grief. She was putting on quite a performance on her own.

Ignoring her plight, the entertainment began and, with 'oohs and aahs' from the audience, Zane walked once and then twice over the postman's body. The tent erupted with admiration and we were all on our feet clapping and cheering - even the postman's girlfriend. Not one to miss a trick, literally, Zane McVain passed around his hat and people were throwing coins in. There was a lone five pound note amongst the mass of change with a piece of paper attached - someone had sketched his face whilst enjoying the show. Zane excitedly retrieved his picture and as he passed around his portrait you could see it had been clearly signed by the cool guy sitting alone in the corner with goatie beard and hat, Damien Hurst.

12th December

Eleven o'clock, Sunday morning and everyone is in bed, including the dog. The hunters are out so that's it for the day - he won't move. In fact he has got a lot better and no longer sits in the shower all day, he will at least just hide behind the hall curtains.

I will have to get him up though, as it has been fourteen hours since he last ventured outside and he must be bursting for a wee. I know I would be. Decided to get ahead with my Christmas cards and get them in the post tomorrow - not too many to do, as I didn't get round to posting half of them last year so they are all ready to go.

My good intentions were shattered however, when out of the blue Maxim and his wife turned up. We had not seen them for ages, so I quickly roused Terry and Ashley from their beds and put the kettle on. Terry said that Maxim had called round earlier in the month and I had missed them. He had given up selling wine by now. as he had been so unwell. He had told me he thought he had understood Maxim's French and that nothing had got lost in the translation, when Maxim had informed Terry that he had broken his balls.

"What do you mean?" I had asked.

"His balls, his testicles," he told me, 'j'ai cassé un testicule' that's what he said I swear."

"What on earth did you say?" I asked, intrigued.

"I don't know, I was a bit embarrassed it's not the sort of thing you normally hear is it?" Terry said.

"I suppose not," I said, "how on earth did he do that that?"

"I have no idea and I certainly didn't want to ask him!"

We both tried to work out how this injury could have occurred. Then I remembered my last conversation with his wife when she had called round in November and we had been shopping together.

"I get depressed," she had said, with her husky Parisian accented voice, "the Normans hate me I have no friends and no job, so I have made some new friends on this superb site for lonely women on the internet, you know Karin?"

I didn't know, but I got where she was coming from. She told me that she had been speaking to people online and how she was enjoying it. Someone had sent her some photos and she showed them to me on her phone. A few were a little raunchy and I said they were a bit sexy didn't she think? I mean half-naked pouting women on your phone - I'm sure that is not normal behaviour for a thirty-nine year old wife and mother. I could be wrong? Exhaling great clouds of smoke all over me. she said that Maxim didn't like it, he thought she was flirting and that there was more to it, so he had banned her. The only time she could do it now was when he was in bed, and she had taken to creeping downstairs when she knew he was sound asleep. She asked me if I had a web cam? Where was this going I thought to myself? Is she a sexually frustrated sex kitten?

I told her to be careful, not everyone is who you think, on the world wide web. She said she had arranged to meet Sylvia, her new friend - the woman on her phone, in Carrefour at St Lo next week for a chat and coffee.

"You think I'm bad Karin? I just need some desire, and Maxim is rubbish, he's so crazy in the head, even the doctor he says, Maxim you have the stress." Anyway, something had broken Stefan's balls, even if it wasn't his wife.

I filled our cups with hot coffee, its aroma fighting for a place with the clouds of cigarette smoke that was permeating the kitchen, I thought how good it was to see them, but unfortunately neither was well. Are all the French hypochondriacs? Jacqueline had been having problems with her heart, (falling in love on the net?) and Maxim was depressed about being out of work and was fed up being at home. Oh and Jacqueline had accidentally run over another of their dogs. They were both on Prozac and various other medications including it seemed forty Marlboro a day and copious amounts of wine. He had a lot of stock left over. All in all it was quite a subdued visit and we didn't like to ask him if his balls were fully recovered. It somehow would have been insensitive.

14th December

Terry and I had a blazing row last night. We don't argue very often but when we do, mount Vesuvius would be proud of me. He was being really difficult and telling me I had to 'downsize', which basically meant throwing out my stuff. I didn't mind doing this with things that I didn't use, but I was saving the doll's house he had made for Sarah, all the Lego we had accumulated and Mathew's Duplo. I have none of Matthew's clothes, not even his old teddy bear, as he was buried with it, that and his comfort blanket 'blankie' and his dummies. He was addicted to the things; if he had grown up I think he would have been a heavy smoker, as he just had to have something in his mouth, often two dummies at a time. I had nothing of his, except a lock of his hair, some photos and films and his plastic bricks. I had carried this big box of Duplo around with me everywhere we had moved to since he died. It had been played with by Sarah and then Ashley, and I wasn't adverse to letting visiting friends' children play with it. I simply could not bear to part with it, it reminded me of the good times we had together on the floor, making train tracks and building houses.

Terry had told me, "we can't take everything with us, it won't be as big as here, so you will have to let some things go." I didn't want to let go, if I did what would I have left? It was hard enough as it was, but I was not going to give away the only thing that I had shared with my son that I had left. I know it sounds really stupid, but that is how I felt. I was being pushed to do something I didn't want to do and I was having a paddy about it.

It was only later that I realised my tantrum had nothing to do with the children's' old toys, that was just an excuse, it was the idea of moving to Greece that was the crux of the matter. My heart was not in it and I was digging in my heels, even if I wasn't admitting it to myself, let alone Terry.

15th December

Picked up Mum, Dad and Auntie Jayne from the airport. They were all very excited and looking forward to a nice relaxing holiday, my Mum didn't stop talking all the way from the airport - no wonder my Dad pretends he's deaf.

I have decided not to mention Greece to Terry, or talk about it to anyone else. I am sort of in denial and am pretending it is just not happening, otherwise I will only end up getting all upset and agitated, having an argument and ruining everybody's Christmas. This would be a new one for me to learn to keep my mouth shut, not bite and try to be polite to everyone – I don't think I have bought myself enough gin.

Good news though, my costume has arrived. The only problem is that now everyone is here for Christmas, when am I going to get a chance to wear it and surprise Terry? My Mum and Dad were following my every move so I had little chance of even trying it on, let alone seeing Terry's reaction. Perhaps I should have saved the twenty-nine dollars (plus post and packing) and just have taken him out for a drink. It certainly didn't look like it did on the website, and I wasn't sure how the hell I would fit into it. I really do think they might have sent me the wrong size. Anyway, it would be difficult enough with the house full to bursting to be intimate anyway. I warned Terry that sex might be off the menu until everyone had left. Terry said, "I don't know what you are on about, your Mum has spent the last six months listening to her neighbour having sex, so I don't think she will mind if we have a go."

18th December

Whilst Terry is picking up my brother and his kids, us ladies are off to the English carol service. It's at the Catholic Church, but you can't be choosey when you are in a foreign country. A sing-song is a sing-song; we would just ignore the service. Still not had a chance to get 'Seven of Nine' out, but I wasn't going to give up hope.

19th December

Sophie has arrived. Her mum dropped her off and she came in for a cup of coffee and a chat. I asked her if they would be doing anything special for Christmas and New Year, she told me they have a big meal on Christmas Day then a huge family party on Boxing Day, (they don't call it that though). They would then have another big meal with fireworks on Saint-Sylvestre (New Year's Eve to us), although, she explained they had given up on the fireworks, as last year a stray rocket managed to land in the hedge close to the house and burnt the whole bush down. Her neighbour still wasn't speaking to her.

Sophie was staying for a few days then going home for Christmas Day and then back again before returning to Ireland. It was good to see her; she looks so well and it's obvious that the Irish air has done her the world of good as she even has a little colour in her cheeks. We all had lunch and then decided to take Sam for a walk. Ashley climbed a tree and managed to get me an enormous bunch of mistletoe. Magically, just as we started to come home, tiny snowflakes started to fall from the sky.

Dad and Terry got the logs in, whilst Mum and Auntie Jayne heated up the mince pies they had made earlier and we put the telly on to watch the Coronation Street omnibus. Needless to say, my brother told us what rubbish we were watching and sloped off to Terry's cinema to watch a film about The New World Order.

I asked Sophie what television programmes she had been watching in Ireland and she replied Sponge Bob and Jeremy Kyle but she thought Jeremy Kyle was a prick. I commented that she had been learning some colourful new words whilst away and she replied, yeah she had, those arseholes on the telly had taught her them. You can just imagine it, au pairs all around the world learning the nuances of the English language via Jeremy Kyle, it didn't bear thinking about.

21st December

Finally got round to Googling Dinner for One and, as I was watching it on YouTube, Mum came over. She told me she had seen it before and that it was Freddy Frinton. He was a comic and she and Dad had seen him at Coventry Palladium years ago. He always played a drunk and had a bent cigarette in his mouth, "Why on earth would the Germans watch it on New Year's Eve? It seems so bizarre," I said, bewildered. We watched it and then I showed it to Terry, it was quite funny, well very funny really and at least we were now prepared for Dinner for One when we visited Brigitte and Wolfgang.

Emailed everyone I had forgotten to send cards to, I made up an excuse, saying that I had been suffering with the flu. My brother said I should have just said I was helping to save the planet. I must remember that one for next year - just think, no more buying cards, writing them and then forgetting to post them. Shame I can't do that with presents (have I been married too long to a Yorkshire man?).

22nd December

Had a good chat with Annie. She had finished work for the holidays and was going out with her new bloke tonight. She was fizzing with excitement, as she had only just met him, so the sex was great. He was very good and had taught her some new and interesting techniques. She had splashed out, going to La Senza for some naughty knickers and had even bought a book on tantric sex (she must like him). She thought this one could be Mr Right and, after thirteen years, she had certainly had her share of Mr Wrongs. Looks like she was in for a happy sex-mas.

Told her about my Star Trek costume and that I hadn't had time to try it out yet as we had a houseful. She said that if it were her, she would just go for it, lock the bedroom door and sod the lot. She told me "You deserve a bit of fun and Terry would love it. He would be made up that you have made the effort." I felt quite spurred on after this; I would get the wine out, make sure everyone had too much to drink and give it a go this very night. I wished her and the boys a happy Christmas and said I would call when she got back from her Christmas trip.

Ashley and Sophie had gone to visit some friends and would not be back until the morning. The rest of us had a lovely meal and, as planned, I got the wine out and filled everyone's glasses again and again and again. It was all going so well - in fact it went so well that eventually everyone trotted off to bed, apart from my brother and Auntie Jayne. They had decided to stay up with the remains of a bottle of Calvados and watch an old Alfred Hitchcock film, keeping the fire going in the wood burner.

I excitedly climbed the stairs to the attic bedroom in which we were sleeping, as the house was now bursting at the seams with all the visitors – especially as my Mum refused to share a room with my Dad due to his snoring and bad feet. At least up here nobody could hear us and we would be able to let off a bit of steam. Taking my costume with me, I locked myself into the bathroom and attempted to squeeze into my alter ego.

I had managed to persuade Terry to follow me – urging him not to be long and he said he would be straight up after letting the dog out for a wee and locking the door. I also suspected he would sneak in a last glass of Calvados with my brother. I didn't mind as I would need half an hour to get into the Bacofoil costume I had stupidly bought. I did feel rather naughty and a little bit sexy, knowing how much he would enjoy seeing me dressed as his fantasy Star Trek character.

As I struggled to get into my costume, I suddenly heard muffled sounds and shouting. The smoke alarm on the landing had gone off, but I was not worried. I knew Terry was still downstairs and would sort it out and, anyway, I was in no position to help with my bum failing to fit into my spray on leggings. I was bouncing around the bedroom with one buttock cheek in and one out - I was on a mission now, I would have to do a lot of wriggling, writhing, jumping and spinning about, but I was determined to get into this bloody outfit, even if it killed me.

I was luckily oblivious to the mayhem that was unravelling downstairs; my brother had managed to set fire to the rug in the lounge and in a state of panic auntie Jayne threw her Calvados on it, igniting it further, Sid had carried it through the house, finally dropping it in the hall, tripping over the dogs bone, setting fire to the dog's bed and startling Terry and the dog in the process.

As Terry struggled to find the back door key the fire was getting out of control. The hall curtains went up, along with the Christmas tree and decorations. It was time to get everyone out the house and call the Pompiers.

Meanwhile, I was blissfully unaware of what was going on. I could hear a lot of noise, but had no idea how serious it was and anyway I had only just got the bottom half of my outfit on. I was now determined to fit into the rest of it.

"COME ON YOU FUCKER, FIT!" I screamed through gritted teeth as I tugged and tugged at the Teflon monstrosity I was struggling to squeeze into, wishing I had ordered the XXXL size.

I went back into the bathroom wondering where Terry was, but thanking God I had been given more time to complete my transformation. At this rate I would be ready and waiting for him when he finally made it up the stairs. After struggling some more and doing a great impression of the dog scratching his bum while moving across the carpet, I had made it! I was in the Seven of Nine costume at last! Looking in the long mirror, though, I felt I looked more like Three out of Ten. But if I lay on the bed in a seductive pose and didn't move I might just get away with it and, if it was anything like our wedding night, then my attire would not remain on for long. God in hell knows how he was going to remove it though? Perhaps I should shout to him and tell him to bring a knife, just in case.

Before I could do this, and without any warning, the large attic window burst open and two startled Pompiers crawled through and grabbed hold of me, pulling me through the window and manhandling me down the ladder outside to the garden. At last I realised what all the noise had been about - the house was on fire!

"Oh my god, what the hell happened?" my husband asked me, "are you hurt? Did you get burnt?" he enquired sympathetically, as he took in the sight of me in my costume, which had now burst at the seams and meant I was fighting to try and cover my dignity. He thought I was wearing one of those silver foil heat blankets, like they give accident victims and marathon runners. I couldn't help myself and after grabbing the towel my mum was offering, I said lying, "yes I inhaled the smoke and they had to wrap me in protective foil!"

"Thank God you're okay. I wondered what the hell had happened to you!" he shrieked. I tried to come up to you but the Pompiers wouldn't let me in insisting it was too dangerous. I knew you'd be OK as long as you didn't come down from the attic," he explained reassuringly.

"Hey sis, what you been up to you look like a tin of sardines," Sid Laughed.

"That reminds me," mum said, "do you think we have enough tin foil for the turkey?"

23rd December

Surprisingly the fire damage is minimal and the house has recovered well. Terry and Sid had got it under control before the fire brigade arrived, so it was mainly the smell and smoke that had transformed my once fairy grotto into a charred mess. Terry realizing in order to make an insurance claim we would need a report from the professionals, so he phoned the Pompiers, just to be on the safe side.

Mum had been scavenging in the bushes and found a nice branch, which we have decorated and put ivy, holly and laurel all over the house. Apart from the burnt rug and curtains the rest has survived without too much mess. My Dad was up the ladder at six o'clock this morning touching up the paintwork and he had Mum cleaning the kitchen from top to bottom. The dog was a bit put out and spent five hours looking with disdain at the new bed I had made him, only giving up and lying on it when he was about to fall over with exhaustion.

No one was hurt, which is the main thing and at least the Pompiers were able to take the opportunity to sell us their annual calendar. They didn't like my suggestion that next year they might like to do a naked one, like they do in England. I think after they found me in my outfit they are convinced that we Brits are sex mad and crazy. They do have a point.

Did the last of the big food shops. I think we have just about covered all bases and have something for everyone, there certainly isn't room for any more food and it looks like I'm opening up my own branch of Waitrose.

I had managed to get everything on the list:

Prawns and Martini for my Mum; cakes and beer for my Dad; pizza and Coke for Ashley; mashed potatoes (instant) and grenadine for Sophie and Sherry (or as near as you can get) for Auntie Jayne who would also like some Brazil nuts, if they have them, if not Turkish Delight will do; organic milk for my brother and more beer, more chocolate, lemonade, orange juice and sparkling water for his kids; Gin, tonic, vodka and brandy for me and any alcohol (preferably over forty-percent proof) beer, wine and four packets of tobacco for Terry.

After Terry had picked himself up off the floor when I told him how much I had spent, he decided to start on the drinks and was going around fixing everyone their desired tipple, this small act of kindness always cheers him up.

I said that I didn't know what he was worried about, it's 2012 next year and, according to my brother (and the Mayan's), it's the end of the world, so I'm not really bothered. The bank would have to chase me for my overdraft and who needs a good credit rating if we are all living in bunkers eating dog food?

Terry said I had been spending too much time listening to my brother and if it really was going to be the end of the world in 2012 then he would shoot himself. At least I would get the insurance pay out I thought.

We had bought Sam a big juicy bone for Christmas, to stop him stealing everyone's slippers and eating them. As Christmas was still a few days away I suggested that we give it to him now, as he had been spotted running across the lawn with Auntie Jayne's knickers in his mouth, I must tell her to keep her bedroom door shut.

We were just putting away the shopping and trying to find new places to hide all the booze before Terry found it and drank it all, when we heard a car pulling up in the drive,

"Who is that?" mum said.

"It's an English car, it's a mini, a black mini cooper, my God it's Sarah, Sarah and her boyfriend!"

We all ran outside ecstatic.

"What are you doing here?" I shouted, as everyone was saying their hellos.

"You didn't think that we would have missed this for the world, did you?" Sarah said smiling, "oh and I forgot to post everyone's Christmas presents, so we thought we would bring them in person."

"Yeah, and there's no food in the flat," her boyfriend added pulling his Marshall Amp out of the car boot.

"I don't want any presents" I carried on, "you being here is the best present in the world. Come here and let me give you a big hug."

"You won't want these Take That tickets then," she teased.

Christmas Eve December 24th

Everyone is here; Terry, Sam, Ashley and Sophie, Sarah and her boyfriend - not to mention Slash the Bearded Dragon, Mum and Dad, my Auntie Jayne and my brother Sid, whose three children arrived this morning.

As we sit with the glow of fairy lights and candles dancing around the room, the smell of wood smoke from the fire, and my special Christmas edition pot pourri, everyone looked content. Even Sam is lying by the fire chewing his giant bone and behaving rather well, for now.

The dinner has been eaten and cleared away. We are all happy and full, having consumed too much. It is the most wonderful sight - all my family in one place, all together, bliss.

"This is it," I said to Terry - the drink giving me the Dutch courage to broach the subject, "this is all I ever wanted, to feel part of a big loving family enjoying special times together. I don't want to give that up, I don't think I can go to Greece. I know I'm letting you down, but I am fed up with being lonely and I want to see my family more often - twice a year is just not enough, " I pleaded, as the tears started to fill my eyes.

"I know, you silly thing. When you were busy cooking dinner the phone rang, it was Brigitte. She and Wolfgang arrive tomorrow with Jenny and they have invited us to go and see Dinner for One with them on New Year's Eve. Oh, and she has sold our house - Happy Christmas Karen."

"But I just said I can't do it, I don't want to be an ex-pat anywhere anymore. I want to go home, I'm sorry Terry but I really can't move to Greece."

"I know that too, I've known for a while and seeing you here with all your family, you are so lucky, we would be mad to leave all this."

"So what are you saying - that we should stay here in France?" I questioned, puzzled by his reply.

"No, it's time to go back home," he said taking my hand.

"But I promised you, and you said even if I didn't want to go you would go anyway and that we would have to separate. I know that you can't face going back to England after all these years."

"I want to be with you," he said, "and if you and I can only be together by being in England, then that's what we will do. I love you Karen and all I want is for us to be happy. You make me happy and without you I am lost and alone."

"But what will we do?" I sobbed.

"We'll figure it out, we always have done before. You know we won't fall off the end of the earth and, if we do, we will have a bloody good laugh getting there."

"I feel like I have let you down, changing my mind and not knowing what I wanted or being honest and pretending to go along with your plans. I'm so sorry."

"Don't be sorry. I understand it has been hard on you and seeing you so happy with all your family to fuss over, well, it sort of reinforces why I'm with you. I love you so much and I never want to be parted from you. I know you tried, but you had to be true to yourself. You had no choice and at least now you know what you do want and what is important to you. I really do respect the consequences of your decision," he said after filling our glasses, "it's a woman's prerogative."

He took my face in his hands and kissed me softly. It felt just like that first kiss we had shared all those years ago in North Devon, on a balmy summer's night with the sky ablaze with stars and the gentle breeze sweeping in off the sea, then walking home tipsily and giddily falling in love, whilst winding our way down dog shit alley.

Coming Soon

Making It In France

Out Spring 2013

About the Author

Karen Bates lives in France with her husband and Golden Retriever called Sam. There are three books in the series and she is currently busy writing the second of the series, titled 'Making It In France'...

9 781781 766378